WINSLOW HOMER, American Artist: His World and His Work

THE LOOKOUT — "ALL'S WELL"

WINSLOW HOMER

AMERICAN ARTIST: HIS WORLD AND HIS WORK

BY

ALBERT TEN EYCK GARDNER

BRAMHALL HOUSE: NEW YORK

McCLELLAN'S CAVALRY

This edition published by Bramhall House, a division of Clarkson N. Potter, Inc.

(B)

The process illustrations were printed by Tipografia Toso, Turin, Italy,
from letterpress plates engraved by Zincotipia Altimanni, Milan, Italy.
The text is set in Bodoni, and printed in Lithography.

Designed by A. Christopher Simon

To Lizzie with Love

ACKNOWLEDGMENTS

No one can write a book about Winslow Homer without acknowledging a deep indebtedness to his two biographers, William Howe Downes and Lloyd Goodrich, Director of the Whitney Museum of American Art. The author's thanks are also due to all the private collectors and museums that have so generously allowed their paintings to be reproduced here.

The author wishes to thank the following publishers for permission to quote from their books:

Crown Publishers, Inc.
The Journal of Eugene Delacroix, translated and edited by Walter Pach. New York, 1948.

Doubleday & Co., Inc.
The Goncourt Journals by Edmond & Jules DeGoncourt. Copyright 1937 by Doubleday & Co., Inc., reprinted by permission of the publisher.

Harper & Brothers
Rogers, W. A. — *A World Worth While*. New York, 1922.

The Macmillan Co.
Lloyd Goodrich — *Winslow Homer*. 1944.

The Museum of Modern Art
Rewald, John — *The History of Impressionism*.

Yale University Library
Weir, John F., manuscript autobiography in the Yale Memorabilia Collection of the Yale University Library.

The author offers especial thanks for the unfailing co-operation and helpful assistance given by the reference librarians and print-room curators in the following institutions:

Metropolitan Museum of Art
New York Society Library
Frick Art Reference Library
New York Public Library
New York Historical Society
Boston Public Library

TABLE OF CONTENTS

LIST OF ILLUSTRATIONS

Color

Black and White

PREFACE

Iɴ 1959 the Metropolitan Museum of Art opened the largest and most comprehensive exhibition of the work of the famous American painter Winslow Homer. This widely heralded exhibition was organized by John Walker, Director of the National Gallery of Art in Washington, and was shown there before coming to New York. In this highly rewarding co-operation between the two museums the Metropolitan Museum provided the introductory essay for the *Winslow Homer Exhibition Catalogue*. This introduction was written by Albert TenEyck Gardner, Associate Curator of American Art. The essay he composed was immediately recognized by many authorities on American Art as an important and significant contribution to the critical writings on Winslow Homer. Mr. Gardner has now expanded this work by the addition of much new material, and the result is the admirable text for this handsomely illustrated volume. This book provides in words and pictures, for the layman as well as for the student of American art and American history, a new view of the life and work of one of our greatest artists by placing him and his work in relation to the main stream of American cultural history.

In the past the Metropolitan Museum has held a number of exhibitions of the work of Winslow Homer. In fact the first really large one-man show of Homer's work was organized by this museum in 1911, just fifty years ago, as a memorial to the artist. This exhibition made available to our visitors for the first time the superb group of watercolors that Homer had set aside for the Metropolitan Museum as a collection that would represent his best work. For a number of years the museum had been negotiating with the artist for the purchase of these pictures, and though Homer refused to part with them he faithfully held them in reserve and they were subsequently purchased by the Metropolitan from his estate. In 1909 Homer wrote to Bryson Burroughs, then Assistant Curator of Paintings:

"The watercolors that you refer to are still hanging on my wall — I think of you and the Museum when I happen to look at them and I never forget that I have promised to submit them to you before offering them to any other party . . . I am not in any hurry and I am sure to notify you.
Respectfully,
Winslow Homer."

The Metropolitan Museum has acquired over the years a really impressive collection of pictures by Homer. While some have been bought, many have been the gifts of generous friends of the Museum. The artist holds such a high place in the history of American art and in the esteem of the general public that the Museum believes he merits an unusually full representation in our collections. The Metropolitan is now able to show the student important examples of every phase of his work. Winslow Homer stands in the small select group of the very best American artists of his time, and his paintings have always been prized by museums and collectors. Homer's famous painting — perhaps his most famous, *The Gulf Stream* — has been on exhibition in our galleries ever since it was purchased in 1906. Today this haunting picture still has a powerful attraction in spite of strong competition from old masters and new. With the passage of time Homer himself has been transformed into an American old master.

The Homer Exhibition of 1959, the catalogue of the exhibition, and this book, which in a special sense owes its existence to that exhibition, all stand as good evidence of the manner in which the Metropolitan endeavors to encourage and promote the study and enjoyment of the art of our own people.

James J. Rorimer, Director
Metropolitan Museum of Art

Cooper Union

THE FISHING PARTY (study)

WINSLOW HOMER, American Artist: His World and His Work

Cooper Union Museum

HOME, SWEET HOME

CHAPTER ONE

PROPOSING A NEW VIEW OF HOMER

"No man can quite emancipate himself from his age and country, or produce a model in which the education, the religion, the politics, usages and arts of his time shall have no share. Though he were never so original, never so wilfull and fantastic, he cannot wipe out of his work every trace of the thoughts amidst which it grew . . . Above his will and out of his sight he is necessitated by the air he breathes and the idea on which he and his contemporaries live and toil, to share the manner of his times."

EMERSON *Art*

THIS BOOK is not an attempt to produce a new standard *Life* of the artist — a task so admirably performed by Lloyd Goodrich. It is an attempt to see Homer's work and his life from a somewhat different, perhaps a broader, point of view than the one a biographer may find himself confined to by necessity or convention. This is an attempt to see Homer and his wonderful pictures in close relation to his time, and to trace in his work the significant and formative effect upon it of the modern art enthusiasms and influences of that time. For these were the influences that Homer selected, adapted, and fused with his great natural talents and his inborn taste into his own individual style. A style consciously developed, perfectly organized, and enlivened by his unique personality — and by this personal distinction, this native talent, this natural taste, his work comes ultimately tuned up to the unmistakable note of genius.

Though Homer's career spans almost exactly the years of Queen Victoria's era, it somehow is not quite possible to think of him as an old-fashioned artist. He is not one of those painters of the nineteenth century whose works were long forgotten and only recently resurrected; revalued perhaps more for their gentle charm and their reminders of the quaint rusticities of a bygone day than for any really superior artistic qualities to be found in them. Winslow Homer is definitely not a painter of this class. He was, and in some mysterious way he remains, a perennially vital modern artist in exactly the same way that some of his French contemporaries remain lively and apparently ageless. Homer seems to win the same kind of active appreciation that is accorded to Manet, Monet, and Degas, Cézanne and Renoir. It is indeed curious that, although the subject matter of their pictures may perhaps appear old-fashioned or be dated by details of costume or topography, the spirit of these men, their approach, their attitude of mind, their range and perception, is not outmoded; their feelings and ideas are immediately communicated to us without our making any allowances for their age. Very few American artists of the nineteenth century have been able to achieve this remarkable, this enviable, estate; in fact Winsow Homer may perchance stand almost alone in his possession of this unusual power through the force and originality of his personality. For it is in large part the reflection of this tough, resiliant, and lively individual character that lights his work with its unique quality and its air of contemporaneity.

In looking at Homer's pictures it is often valuable to recall in imagination the work of some of the other American painters of the late nineteenth century and to contrast them, in our mind's eye, with Homer's paintings. It is only in this way that one can fully realize just how much he rose above most of them and how far aside from some of the fashionable currents in the American art world he stood as an independent Yankee. It seems that even some of the so-called "big names" of the Nineties cannot now stand close comparison with Homer. And of these big names perhaps the very biggest in American art at that time would be James Abbott McNeill Whistler. Perhaps time has been unusually cruel to Mr. Whistler in demonstrating inexorably how very wide the gulf can be between the happy accidents of the inspired artistic dilettante and the solid, controlled mastery of the professional painter. Many another popular artist of the time can now be thought of only as one of the almost-forgotten extras, the spear carriers who flash momentarily in the background of the grand opera of art history. Their pictures illustrate old-fashioned attitudes of mind toward life and art; age makes them seem merely antiquated without giving them grace or dignity. Thus it is with something like surprise that we realize that it is now more than a hundred years since Homer stood, as a young man of twenty-one, upon the threshold of his career with all his triumphs lying dormant in the unknown future, awaiting his touch to bring them to life.

Homer's reputation as one of the most important American artists of his time has never really suffered any perceptible decline, and the great esteem in which he was held in his later life remained

Brooklyn Museum

SHOOTING THE RAPIDS

ON A LEE SHORE

THE BRIDLE PATH, WHITE MOUNTAINS

THE BERRY PICKERS

more or less constant in the years after his death. Now with the passage of half a century his reputation is clearly rising to new heights, and appreciation of his work is spreading to new generations of admirers. Many a puissant name in the world of art fails to survive the neglect or changes in taste that make this period of fifty years such a crucial test in the life of a painter's reputation. In most cases the living personality of the artist — his own unique charm and warm heart — are most important elements in the establishment and maintenance of his position during his lifetime, and when these can no longer operate to illumine and perhaps magnify the value of his paintings, the pictures sink into a sort of twilight zone of half-forgotten things, things that are unable to make their way against the competition of new men, new times, new ideas. But this fate has never overtaken Winslow Homer. Perhaps because he cut himself off from most social contacts in mid-career — in his later years he never appeared at exhibition teas, gallery receptions, or varnishing days, and in some instances he refused to send paintings to the big annual shows in which most painters were so anxious to be represented — perhaps, also, because he withdrew from the community of artists into the seclusion of the Maine coast long before his death, his pictures always had to make their own way in the world without much assistance from him. At least the kind of assistance that would involve the artist in any of the public social functions.

But Homer's pictures, with their strange attractive power, had by themselves alone the strength to make very definite impressions whenever they were shown, without depending to any degree on the kind of support that the personal charm of the artist can give to his work. Homer's pictures were always impossible to ignore — so bold, perhaps even harsh, was their forthright statement of purpose. They never needed an apologist to explain or excuse; they spoke for themselves with such a simple clarity that no interpreter was needed. And today because of this power, this clarity and force, in spite of the colorful stridency of much modern painting, Homer's pictures, in competing with them, still deliver their message with undiminished vitality, and his abstractions of the sea can compete on almost equal terms with some of the abstractions of today.

Though some of Homer's pictures have to a marked degree this note of modernity, time has brought to many of them a mellowing air of familiarity that makes them seem to us like old friends, comfortably at ease in a silent, understanding companionship. In recent years so many of his pictures have been given wide circulation as color reproductions it is probably safe to say that printed copies of Homer's work today are admired by thousands of people as opposed to the perhaps mere hundreds who saw his original paintings in exhibitions during his lifetime. The new processes for making color reproductions of painting — particularly of watercolor paintings — so accurately reproduce the feeling of the originals that when they are printed on rough watercolor paper it is virtually impossible to tell that they are reproductions made by mechanical means, unless they are subjected to the closest inspection. By these mechanical means Homer now has a much larger circle of admirers than he ever had before, and reproductions of his work can now be found everywhere.

Apparently his pictures continue effortlessly to win from new generations of critics the same kind of ardent friends they won long ago, friends who unhesitatingly recognize his sterling merit as a designer of pictures, friends who now discover in his work new virtues and hitherto-unsuspected qualities that may have been obscured from some of his unperceptive contemporaries, some of whom thought his work barbarically crude and forthright. These newly seen qualities and once-unappreciated virtues now seem to rise in value and to assume their truly important place as vital basic elements of his own personal style, elements always controlled by his own peculiar genius, elements that have always given his work its distinctive and enduring character, elements that have inevitably set Homer apart from the whole body of his fellow American artists. It is the continual renewal of the appreciation of these things that has prevented his work from falling into obscurity, and it is

SCHOONERS AT ANCHOR, KEY WEST

SUNLIGHT ON THE COAST

WINTER COAST

these same things that continue to elevate and sustain him in his present position of eminence in the history of American painting.

Since 1910, when Homer died, scarcely a decade has passed without at least one important exhibition of his work. In 1911 the Metropolitan Museum of Art opened a special loan exhibition in memory of the artist, an exhibition arranged with the co-operation of Homer's brother Charles and other members of the Homer family. That same year a memorial exhibition of his work was held at the John Herron Art Institute in Indianapolis. In celebration of the hundredth anniversary of his birth four major exhibitions were held. In 1936 there was a "century loan exhibition" in Homer's studio at Prouts Neck, Maine, and that same year a large special exhibition of Homer's paintings was held in the Philadelphia Museum of Art. The following year a memorable exhibition of Homer's work was held at the Whitney Museum of American Art, and another exhibition marked his hundredth anniversary at the Carnegie Institute in Pittsburgh. In 1945 a group of Homer watercolors was exhibited in the art museums in Minneapolis, Detroit, and Brooklyn. In 1951 the Smith College Art Museum at Northampton, Massachusetts, held an exhibition titled *Winslow Homer: Illustrator*, an exhibition that reflected the growing awareness of a phase of his early work, which had been arousing

Phillips Collection

TO THE RESCUE

Wadsworth Athenaeum, Hartford, Connecticut

ROCKY COAST

Mr. and Mrs. Charles S. Payson

WEATHERBEATEN

more and more interest. The most comprehensive showing of Homer's work, however, was the exhibition organized by the National Gallery of Art in Washington in 1958, an exhibition that was later displayed at the Metropolitan Museum of Art in New York, and still later, in somewhat modified form, at the Boston Museum of Fine Arts.

Each one of these exhibitions has been inevitably responsible for arousing new interest in the artist, and in many cases this interest has resulted in new accounts of Homer's life and reconsideration of various aspects of his work. This steady production over the last fifty years of appreciative critical and biographical literature about the artist and his pictures attests the unflagging public and scholarly interest in him.

This interest, beginning of course on a modest scale early in his career, has continued slowly but steadily to increase, without any important interruption, right down to the immediate present. And if we may judge from these indications, it is an interest that will be prolonged into the indefinite future. For Winslow Homer has by now achieved his permanent place in American painting, a place of honor that he will surely keep. He has in his own way become one of the great standard monuments in the history of American art. Few other American painters have managed so adroitly to capture and retain in quite the same measure the lively appreciation accorded to him. It was Homer's skill in continuously producing paintings of such impressive merit, of such individual character, that critical attention as well as popular notice and approbation inevitably singled out his pictures for special comment, commendation, or occasionally for complaint whenever his work was placed on exhibition.

In 1914 the painter Kenyon Cox wrote a book on Homer, and in a prefatory note he hints that every conceivable comment about the artist had already been made. But that this was manifestly untrue was proved by the publication in 1944 of Lloyd Goodrich's definitive biography of Homer, a

Museum of Fine Arts, Boston

THORNHILL BAR

book that finally collected and marshaled every known fact about the artist. This is an indispensable work to which every student of Homer is deeply indebted. In all probability very little new biographical material about Homer will turn up to be added to the record, and now there is not much that is new that can be said about his personal life.

In view of all this it may seem very bold to attempt yet another word on the artist. However, the inescapable fact remains that as Homer and his epoch recede deeper and deeper into the past, and as new generations of viewers rise to become subject to the spell his paintings still exert, it may not be without value, perhaps it may even be necessary, to review from time to time the work of the man who in his lifetime so deeply impressed his contemporaries that they called him without equivocation "the greatest American artist" — "the most American painter" — "the most intensely American painter of his time." Any artist who wins and holds such resounding titles of honor from the critics, from the public, and from his fellow artists must inevitably be the subject of reappraisal and re-examination by each new generation of students of American art and American life.

In reading the standard accounts of Homer's life it is indeed amazing to find how really scanty the record is, and to find that he was so reticent about himself and his ideas about art that his biographers have been unable to discover many detailed records to complement and illumine his life as recorded in his paintings. In fact we probably know more about the lives of some artists of the Renaissance than we know about the life of Homer. But this is apparently the way he wanted it to be, as we know from his letter to his first biographer, William Howe Downes, a letter in which Homer

Fogg Museum of Art

HOMOSASSA JUNGLE IN FLORIDA

absolutely refused to supply Downes with any personal information. Homer felt, and his feelings on the point were expressed in no uncertain terms, that his private life was of absolutely no concern to those who looked at his pictures. Perhaps Homer wished to leave his paintings as the only true records of his life. In any case, by doing this he has made it certain that they will be most carefully studied. Thus, without detailed autobiography, without journals, diaries, or reminiscences, and with only a few brief letters, the student is forced again and again to fall back on the sole direct evidence remaining to us — the paintings themselves.

In Homer's life there are several important periods about which very little is known, and for information on these interesting times it is necessary to examine with the most careful attention the paintings and drawings Homer produced then. Unfortunately the drawings of his childhood and youth, which would reveal his early tendencies and enthusiasms, have been destroyed, and his work as an apprentice lithographer conformed, at the demand of his employer, rather closely to the current commercial conventions, so that while it may show his technical skill it is without much value as a personal record. Other periods of obscurity occur when Homer was in Europe — first in 1867, when he spent almost a year in Paris, and second in 1881–82, when he lived near Tynemouth in England. Judging from his pictures and from the events of the time, it is certain that important things happened to Homer during each of these rather irritatingly mysterious periods in his career. It would seem that his trip to Paris when he was thirty-one had the most important effect on his work, whereas his stay near Tynemouth when he was forty-five marked some significant turning point in his personal

New Britain Museum of American Art

A SKIRMISH IN THE WILDERNESS

SCHOONER AT SUNSET

life, for it resulted in his withdrawal from New York, where he had been a fairly well-known member of the art world, and his retirement to the isolation of a small summer resort on the coast of Maine. Without any question, however, the most important of these curiously blank periods in Homer's career is the ten months he spent in Paris when he was just beginning to establish his reputation as a painter.

By reviewing in chronological sequence Homer's illustrations and paintings made in the years 1866–68, before, during, and immediately after his stay in Paris, there are to be found certain clues that may be interpreted to show quite clearly the effect of the new influences to which he was subjected both at home and abroad. His work after his return to New York reveals in quite a positive way that in these years some most important things had happened to him. It reveals the final emergence and consolidation of new patterns of thought, the expression of a distinctive new attitude of mind, the evidence of a new vantage point taken by the artist. The old illustrated-newspaper style that characterized his work before 1867 is scarcely to be seen in it after that date. The effect of his Parisian experiences is no less evident in his painting, and in all his work we see how the tentative experiments and frankly imitative efforts of the talented self-taught illustrator are suddenly matured and transformed into the considered work of an artist with a firm, self-conscious mastery of hand and eye. The effect of what he learned in Paris is plainly evident in all·his subsequent work. It was there, in Paris, that he discovered himself and it was there that he reappraised and adopted

THE SPONGE DIVER, BAHAMAS

BOYS IN A PASTURE

"OLD SETTLERS," ADIRONDACKS

the sound guiding principles that gave final form and direction to his work.

Placing the artistic factors in Homer's work in relation to the variegated background of important currents and influential events that were actively felt in British and French art when Homer was in Europe, we are enabled to examine our artist in an unaccustomed if not an entirely new way. These reveal glimpses and deeper insights into things that caught his eye and spurred his imagination. They make it possible to fill in a number of vitally important facts about the foreign influences that were to be of the utmost significance in the final formation of his individual style.

All of these clues, facts, and background notes lead one to speculate upon Homer's development and to muse upon all the interesting possibilities presented by the contemporary scene, the character of the man himself, and the manners, uses, and enthusiasms of his time. And these speculations and ruminations seem inevitably to terminate in some conclusions about the development of Homer as an artist that differ rather widely from the settled — perhaps too long settled — opinions and conclusions reached by Homer students in the past. The pursuit of the seductive theories suggested by these possibilities — of new relationships between the artist and the main artistic trends that were current during his formative years — will be seen to lead us into an unfamiliar region of relatively unexplored territory in the history of art, especially in the history of American art. Yet it is only by turning our attention in this unaccustomed direction that we can be rewarded with useful and significant insights into the formation of the style of "the most American" artist of the nineteenth century.

Mr. and Mrs. Courtlandt P. Dixon

DEER DRINKING

Cooper Union Museum

CAVALRY OFFICER

A close study of Homer's work allows us to raise factual pillars that support new theories about him, theories that might otherwise have been considered quite fanciful. Perhaps we should no longer resist the temptation to allow our imagination to range freely over the fascinating vistas that are to be opened up for our inspection. However, before venturing forth on this interesting excursion it would be well to place the artist in the enframing circumstances of his time with a brief account of his life.

Cooper Union Museum

THE GULF STREAM (study)

CANNON ROCK

COUNTRY SCHOOL

Museum of Fine Arts, Boston

LONG BRANCH, NEW JERSEY

Museum of Fine Arts, Springfield, Massachusetts

PROMENADE ON THE BEACH

PRISONERS FROM THE FRONT

CHAPTER TWO

BIOGRAPHICAL SKETCHES

"The life that I have chosen gives me my full hours of enjoyment for the balance of my life. The Sun will not rise, or set, without my notice and thanks."

Winslow Homer in a letter to his brother, Charles, written in February 1895.

GOODRICH — *Winslow Homer*

No one has ever succeeded in casting any bohemian glamour on the plain facts of Winslow Homer's biography. In reality the account of his life is not much more than a sober workaday Yankee record of illustrations drawn and published, watercolors and oils painted, exhibited, and sold. Toward the end of his career he received solidly rewarding sums of cash for his work, and the equally satisfying recognition that came from his fellow artists and from the art organizations of the country that honored themselves in awarding to him gold medals and prizes. However, in general his life was a rather quiet one.

One of the difficulties presented to those who would write a biography of Winslow Homer is that the man himself is so elusive. His great reserve, his love of privacy, his self-effacement, while they may be admirable characteristics, leave the biographer with at best a rather shadowy personality to deal with. Homer does not fit well into any ordinary category, he was neither founder nor close follower of any school of painting, in life he stood alone as a man and as an artist, and in history he remains more or less a solitary, and his extreme reticence about his ideas and about his personal life raises many problems. While he could not be called a man of mystery, he was not, even at the high tide of his fame, a popular public personality. His life was not one of those glamorous storybook adventures full of dramatic tensions and unexpected turns of fortune.

A number of his letters have survived, but the majority of them have been preserved by the dealers who sold his pictures; thus the main topic of most of them is the business details of selling pictures — prices, framing, shipping, etc. Though these letters contain a certain amount of information of interest to the biographer, they are not the intimate kind of personal letter addressed to friends or relatives that might tell us more about the man himself. Even the letters he did address to members of his family are in general brief and very revealing. The fragmentary remarks and bits of conversation recorded in various places make up a tantalizing glimpse, but hardly more than a glimpse, of the artist.

From what little has been recorded about Homer's parents we know that both of them were strongly individualistic people with marked personalities of an unusual stamp. The mere fact that Homer's father encouraged him in his desire to be an artist makes the father stand out as a rather unorthodox Victorian parent. His mother's skill as a painter, her love of art, her reputation for wit

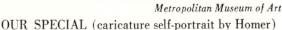

Metropolitan Museum of Art   *Photograph from William Howe Downes*
OUR SPECIAL (caricature self-portrait by Homer)   WINSLOW HOMER

and charm must have inevitably had the most profound influence upon her sons. Homer's paintings, though far from being "literary," disclose to us such a strong, such an all-pervading atmosphere of the superior and detached mind, we must conclude that the Cambridge household in which the Homer boys grew up was, as were so many Cambridge homes of that day, a place where opportunities for serious reading and thinking and for purposeful intellectual exercise were not lacking.

Perhaps every biography of Homer should start with his letter to William Howe Downes, the art critic of the Boston *Transcript*, who proposed to write a book about the artist. In August 1908, Homer wrote: "It may seem ungrateful to you that after your twenty-five years of hard work in booming my pictures I should not agree with you in regard to the proposed sketch of my life. But I think it would probably kill me to have such a thing appear, and, as the most interesting part of my life is of no concern to the public, I must decline to give you any particulars in regard to it."

This letter must be something of a classic document in the history of American art of the time, for Homer must have been almost alone among American painters in his desire for privacy. This tantalizing statement, declining to make public "the most interesting part of my life," has piqued the curiosity of everyone, and perhaps it has cast the sole note of real glamour and mystery over a life that was presumably nothing more than a simple and reasonably happy one — the life of an artist who was content in the occupations and pastimes that pleased him most.

Fogg Museum of Art

PITCHING HORSESHOES

City Art Museum, St. Louis

SKATING IN CENTRAL PARK

Here in very brief form are the essential facts of Homer's biography. He was born in Boston in 1836. Both of his parents were of old New England stock and the artist was the descendant of plain English merchants, seamen, and farmers who settled in the region in the late seventeenth century. His father, Charles Savage Homer, was an importer of hardware. His mother, though she was born in Maine, was brought up in Cambridge. The Homer family group was an exceptionally close-knit unit, and Winslow and his brothers, Charles and Arthur, were close companions. About 1842 the Homer family moved to what was then the rural village of Cambridge, where the boys could play in the nearby fields and woods and fish in the streams and ponds of the neighborhood. At the age of nineteen, after the usual schooling, Winslow's remarkable amateur talents at drawing admitted him to apprenticeship (1855–57) with the lithographer and publisher of prints J. H. Bufford in Boston. At the end of his apprenticeship Homer set himself up as a free-lance illustrator. At this time most of his work consisted of drawings for the popular illustrated magazines. Later he settled in New York (1859), where he continued to work for *Harper's Illustrated Weekly*. About this time, although he was then a successful magazine illustrator, he attended, for a short period, drawing classes in Brooklyn and the night classes of the rather poor little school of the National Academy of Design. At this time he also had some private instruction in painting in oil colors from Frédéric Rondel.

During the Civil War, Homer went as "artist correspondent" a number of times to the battlefields and encampments of Union troops in Virginia. On these excursions he made sketches that were

Mr. and Mrs. Carleton Mitchell

GLOUCESTER HARBOR

GLOUCESTER FARM

THE WATERMELON BOYS

later engraved for *Harper's Weekly*. During the war years he began to experiment with watercolors and oils and to develop in these mediums his war sketches. Some of them were worked into large canvases that could be exhibited at the annual shows of the National Academy of Design. His picture *Prisoners from the Front*, exhibited there in 1866, brought the artist to a new position of prominence and prestige, largely because of the timely nature of his subject matter but partly because of the individual style of his work. The following year he set out on his first trip to Europe. He stayed in Paris for about ten months, for part of that time sharing the studio of his friend the Boston painter Albert Kelsey.

On his return to New York, Homer devoted more and more time to painting and eventually ceased altogether to work for the illustrated magazines (1875). On his next trip to Europe, 1881–82, he stayed at Tynemouth, painting the fisherfolk and the sea. On his return to America he went to Prouts Neck (1883), a small, isolated community on the coast of Maine. This place now became his home, and from there he set out annually on his various hunting, fishing, and sketching trips — in summer to the Adirondacks or Canada, and in winter to Florida and Nassau, Cuba and Bermuda — journeys to the backwoods of the north and to the backwaters of the tropical south, which he recorded in his brilliant series of watercolors; sketches upon which a large part of his present fame rests with such firm security.

At Prouts Neck he studied the somber moods of the sea and translated his findings into the series of large marine paintings, for which he was chiefly noted in his later years. Here he led a progressively more and more solitary life, devoting himself to his garden, his painting, and the contemplation of

Detroit Institute of Arts

DEFIANCE: INVITING A SHOT BEFORE PETERSBURG, VIRGINIA, 1864

CAVALRY OFFICER (sketch)

SOLDIERS' HEADS

A RAINY DAY IN CAMP

the waves and rocks. He died at Prouts Neck in 1910.

In view of the extreme scarcity of biographical material about Homer — that is, material *he* approved for publication during his lifetime — the recent discovery of a letter from him in the archives of the Department of Paintings in the Metropolitan Museum of Art, in which he sends a long biographical sketch and his specific approval of the statements in it, may be considered a major find. In 1907 the Department of Paintings was contemplating the publication of a new catalogue. At that time they wrote to all the living artists whose paintings had been added to the collection since the last edition of the catalogue, requesting biographical information to be included in the new edition. This request for information brought from Homer the following letter:

Scarboro, Maine
July 30th, 1907

Department of Paintings
Metropolitan Museum of Art
Mr. d'Hervilly
Dear Sir:

Enclosed please find a catalogue of the Clarke Sale — in which you will find a notice of my life to date — It is correct in every respect — (I have crossed out the only objection to it).

Yours Very Truly

WINSLOW HOMER

Wadsworth Athenaeum, Hartford, Connecticut

THE NOONING

THANKSGIVING DAY, 1858

With such emphatic approval (the underlined passage was so marked by Homer) and the slight bit of censorship (as will be seen, a few words about money were deleted by Homer) this biographical sketch can now take its place as a prime document in the biography of the artist. The brevity of this sketch, however regrettable that may be, allows us to reprint it here in full with the words about money (which he so primly cut out) put back in their place.

About the middle of the fifties, a youth of nineteen found employment in the establishment of a lithographer in the city of Boston, where he was born in 1836. From the start the young man displayed remarkable aptitude as a draughtsman. He had entered the shop as an apprentice, and remained at work there until he had completed his twenty-first year [and saved a little money out of his wages. On this modest capital], he came to New York, where he entered himself as a student at the National Academy of Design, and became a pupil of Frédéric Rondel, a French artist then in great repute in New York as a teacher. Incidental to his studies, he made illustrations on wood blocks for publishers, by means of which he found it possible to support himself. At the outbreak of the Civil War he went to Washington, making excursions in various directions with the armies, and furnishing drawings of his experiences and the episodes of the war to *Harper's Weekly*. It was at this time that he began to apply his lessons in painting. The subjects he chose were those suggested by the life and scenes around him — scenes of camp and campaign life — the first of them to attract attention being "Prisoners from the Front." This actual scene of the war for the Union, appearing at a time when popular excitement was at fever heat, made a profound impression, and established the painter's reputation immediately. He was made an Associate of the National Academy in 1864, an Academician the following year, and in 1866 assisted in organizing the American Water Color Society. He made his first visit to Europe at this time, but his stay was brief, and his experience, while it enlarged his field of subjects, had no perceptible influence on his individuality. He works now, as he did at the beginning, in utter independence of schools and masters. His method is entirely his own. He was a realist, before realism had become a fixed fact in French art, from which it has since been so extensively imported into our own. He painted nature as he saw it — always, however, seeing it with a lively appreciation of all that is picturesque and dramatic. His command of the local color and spirit of a scene is always masterly, and whether he gives us a group of English fishergirls, a landscape in the Bahamas, a camp of pioneers or fishermen in the wilderness, or a bit of the real life and nature of a Southern plantation or the New England coast, the impression of actuality which he conveys is equally vivid and penetrating. During recent years Mr. Homer has worked most of the

Metropolitan Museum of Art

UNION MEETINGS

time in his studio on the Maine coast, producing, in a series of marine and coast subjects, a series of pictures by which the standard of his art has been established at the head of the American school. He has experimented in etching subjects of his own selection and design, and in this art has executed some plates of an originality and power in correspondence with his works in color.

This biographical and critical account appears to present the artist as he saw himself — or at least as he wished to be seen. It is interesting to note in it his insistence on his complete independence of schools and masters, his desire to be under obligation to no one, and his final advertisement of his etchings with a note of pride. This account would seem to confirm the often-questioned statement that Homer was a founder of the American Water Color Society.

Although in his later years Homer did everything he could to ward off inquiring journalists, art critics, and biographers by flatly refusing to co-operate with them in giving any information about himself or his pictures, there exist two accounts that were based on interviews with the artist. The first of these took place in the spring of 1866, when the young author Thomas Bailey Aldrich visited him in his studio. At this time Homer was just at the beginning of his career and had produced very few paintings, so the importance of this account is somewhat limited and its interest lies principally in the picture it gives of the New York art world as a background for the young artist; therefore, quotations from it are to be found in a subsequent chapter.

Metropolitan Museum of Art

THE HALT OF THE WAGON TRAIN

LIFE IN CAMP (part 1)

The second, and much more informative, interview was given to George W. Sheldon sometime about 1878–79. Two variants of this were published: in the *Art Journal* in 1878–79, and in Sheldon's book *American Artists*, published in 1879. Sheldon also published a number of quotations from Homer in his book *Hours with Art and Artists* issued about 1882. In these little essays Sheldon's critical comments are intermingled with bits of the artist's biography and some very interesting quotations. The importance of the biographical information (as with the account in the Clarke sale catalogue) lies in the fact that all the information about Homer's life and his ideas about art must have come directly from the artist himself. In many respects Sheldon's account outranks in significance both the somewhat limited paper by Aldrich and the Clarke sale catalogue biography. Its importance is enhanced by the fact that it was given to a practicing writer on fine arts, whereas

Aldrich was merely writing an instructive Sunday-school story for children. Since Sheldon's account is one of the most important sources of information about Homer it is worth quoting at some length.

In the spring of 1878 MR. WINSLOW HOMER exhibited in a Boston auctionroom a collection of fifty or more sketches in pencil and in watercolors which possessed unusual interest. In composition they were not remarkable — few of Mr. Homer's productions are noteworthy in that respect; he does not seem to care greatly for it; but, in their ability to make the spectator feel their subjects at once, they are very strong. Some of them were exceedingly simple — a girl swinging in a hammock, another standing in the fields, a third playing checkers or chess — yet from almost all of them there came a sense of freshness and pleasurableness. The handling of the figures was easy and decisive; you said to yourself that the pictures had been made quickly and without effort, and you felt that in most instances, at least, they were true to Nature. When the sale took place they provoked considerable competition, but did not fetch a great deal of money, partly because of the stringency of the times, partly because of the lateness of the season, and partly because of their fragmentary character. They widened and strengthened the artist's reputation, however, displaying his genius to much better advantage than do many of his finished works.

Mr. Homer is, perhaps, as much respected by intelligent lovers of art as is any other painter in this country. He was born in Boston, February 24, 1836. When six years old he went with his parents to Cambridge, and acquired a lasting liking for out-door country-life. The ponds, the meadows, and the fishing became his delight. To this day there is no recreation that he prefers to an excursion

Metropolitan Museum of Art

A BIVOUAC FIRE ON THE POTOMAC

in the country. Like most artists, he was fond of drawing sketches in his boyhood. He has a pile of crayon reproductions of all sorts of things, made as early as 1847, each picture being supplemented by his full name and the exact date, in careful juvenile fashion. His father encouraged his leaning towards art, and, on one occasion, when on a visit to London, sent him a complete set of lithographs by Julian — representations of heads, ears, noses, eyes, faces, trees, houses, everything that a young draughtsman might fancy trying his hand at — and also lithographs of animals by Victor Adam, which the son hastened to make profitable use of. At school he drew maps and illustrated text-books, stealthily but systematically. When the time came for him to choose a business or profession, his parents never once thought of his becoming an artist, and, of course, did not recognize the fact that he was one already. It chanced on a certain morning that his father, while reading a newspaper, caught sight of the following brief advertisement: "Boy wanted; apply to Bufford lithographer. Must

Metropolitan Museum of Art

MAKING HAVELOCKS FOR THE VOLUNTEERS

have a taste for drawing. No other wanted." Now Bufford was a friend of the elder Homer, and a member of the fire company of which the latter was the foreman — in those days the fire department in New England towns was conducted by gentlemen. "There's a chance for Winslow!" exclaimed the author of Winslow's being. Application was made forthwith to Bufford; and the furnishings store across the way, where were sold dickeys etc., and where, at one time, it was seriously thought that Winslow had better begin life as clerk, was abandoned for the headquarters of Cambridge lithography. The boy was accepted on trial for two weeks. He suited, and stayed for two years, or until he was twenty-one. He suited so well, indeed, that his employer relinquished the bonus of three hundred dollars usually demanded of apprentices in consideration of their being taught a trade. His first work was designing title pages for sheet-music, ordered by Oliver Ditson of Boston — "Katy Darling" and

Christmas Boxes in Camp—Christmas, 1861.

Metropolitan Museum of Art

CHRISTMAS BOXES IN CAMP—CHRISTMAS 1861

Mr. and Mrs. Lawrence Fleischman

THE INITIALS

THE VETERAN IN A NEW FIELD

WEANING THE CALF

EARLY MORNING AFTER A STORM AT SEA

INSIDE THE BAR

"Oh, whistle and I'll come to you, My Lad" being the subjects of his initial efforts in this direction. Bufford assigned to him the more interesting kinds of pictorial decoration, leaving such avocations as card-printing to the other apprentices. His most important triumph at the lithographers was the designing on stone of the portraits of the entire Senate of Massachusetts. But his sojourn there was a treadmill existence. Two years at that grindstone unfitted him for further bondage; and, since the day he left it, he has called no man master. He determined to be an artist; took a room in the *Ballou's Pictorial* Building, in Winter Street, Boston, and made drawings, occasionally, for that periodical. His first production there was a sketch of a street-scene in Boston — some horses rearing in lively fashion, and several pedestrians promenading the sidewalk. In a year or two he began to send sketches to Harper and Brothers, of New York, who invariably accepted them. Some of these early works were a series entitled "Life in Harvard College," including a football game on the campus. He knew the students well, and had cultivated them a good deal. Next he drew cartoons of the muster at Concord, in 1857 or 1858 also for the Harpers. Soon he spent a winter in New York, attending a drawing school in Brooklyn, and visited the old Duesseldorf Gallery on Broadway, where he saw and was deeply impressed by Page's "Venus." "What I remember best," says Mr. Homer, "is the smell of paint; I used to love it in a picture-gallery." The Harpers sent for him, and made him a generous offer to enter their establishment and work regularly as an artist. "I declined it," says Homer, "because I had had a taste of freedom. The slavery at Bufford's was too fresh in my recollection to let me care to bind myself again. From the time I took my nose off that lithographic stone, I have had no master, and never shall have any."

It was in 1859 that he came to New York. For two years he occupied a studio in Nassau Street, and lived in Sixteenth Street. Gradually he got acquainted with the artists, and in 1861 he moved to the University Building on Washington Square, where several of them had rooms. He attended the night school of the Academy of Design, then in Thirteenth Street, under Prof. Cummings' tuition, and in 1861 determined to paint. For a month, in the old Dodworth Building near Grace Church, he took lessons in painting of Rondel, an artist from Boston, who once a week, on Saturdays, taught him how to handle his brush, set his palette, etc. The next summer he bought a tin box containing pigments, oils, and various equipments, and started out into the country to paint from Nature. Funds being scarce, he got an appointment from Harpers as artist-correspondent at the seat of war, and went to Washington, where he drew sketches of Lincoln's inauguration, and afterwards to the front with the first batch of soldier-volunteers. Twice again he made a trip to the Army of the Potomac, these times independently of the publishers. His first oil paintings were pictures of war scenes; for example; "Home Sweet Home," which represents homesick soldiers listening to the playing of a regimental band; "The Last Goose at Yorktown," now owned by Mr. Dean of Waverly Place, New York; and "Zouaves Pitching Quoits." In 1865 he painted his "Prisoners from the Front," recently in Mr. John Taylor Johnston's collection, a work which soon gave him reputation.

One of his latest productions is the "Cotton Pickers," two stalwart Negro women in a cotton-field, which now has a home in London. His "A Fair Wind" and "Over the Hills" are in New York, in Mr. Charles Smith's gallery. Mr. Homer is not wholly a master of *technique*, but he understands the nature and the aims of art; he can see and lay hold of the essentials of character, and he paints his own thoughts — not other persons'. It is not strange, therefore, that almost from the outset of his career as a painter, his works have compelled the attention of the public, and have invested themselves with earnest admiration. The praise they have earned is honest praise. They reveal on the part of the artist an ability to grasp dominant characteristics and to reproduce specific expressions of scenes and sitters, and for this reason it is that no two of Mr. Homer's pictures look alike. Every canvas with his name attached bears the reflex of a distinct artistic impression. His style is large and free, realistic and straightforward, broad and bold; and many of his finished works have somewhat of the charm of open-air sketches — were, indeed, painted out-doors in the sunlight, in the immediate presence of Nature; while in the best of them may always be recognized a certain noble simplicity, quietude, and sobriety, that one feels grateful for in an age of gilded-eagleism, together with an abundance of free touches made in inspired unconsciousness of rules, and sometimes fine enough almost to atone for insufficiency of textures and feebleness of relation of color.

STUDIO BUILDING, WEST 10TH STREET, NEW YORK

His Negro studies, recently brought from Virginia, are in several respects — in their total freedom from conventionalism and mannerism, in their strong look of life, and in their sensitive feeling for character — the most successful things of the kind that this country has yet produced. One of them, "Eating Watermelons," we have engraved. It is a chapter in the life of an American boy. His "Snap the Whip" and "Village School," in Mr. John Sherwood's collection, are other chapters. His fame as a painter was founded upon his original and happy treatment of just such subjects as these. "In the Fields" shows us a stalwart young farmer stopping to listen to the song of the lark. "The Song of the Lark" was its title on the occasion of its first exhibition in 1877 in the gallery of the Century Club.

Certain facts in the Sheldon account stand out and they are important keys to the character of the artist, reflecting as they do his independence, his dislike of being tied down to a routine job, his refusal to submit to the grinding drudgery of a regular job as an illustrator for Harper's; and his love for the freedom of the forest, the field, and the sea. These are characteristics that mark not only his life but all of his paintings. Sheldon's critical comments, too, are no less valuable, for he manages to state there in only a few lines an admirable summary of Homer's style — a statement that can hardly be improved. It begins: "His style is large and free, realistic and straightforward, broad and bold . . . in the best of his paintings may always be recognized a noble simplicity, quietude, and sobriety . . . together with an abundance of free touches made in inspired unconsciousness of rules . . ."

In his book *Hours with Art and Artists,* Sheldon quotes a number of Homer's remarks, but since none of them deals with the artist's biography but is concerned with some of his ideas about painting, they will be found in a subsequent chapter.

One of the best complements to the portrait photographs of Winslow Homer is the description of him given in Harrison Morris's *Confessions in Art.* He writes:

It must have been on the trip to Boston for Jury meeting, in this year 1896, that I met Winslow Homer . . . I remember walking along Boylston Street with him . . . He was a slender smallish figure, with red, or nearly red, hair and a great waving mustache of the same color, dated at the year of the Civil War. His garb was of the fashion of the day, black cutaway coat, faultless linen, a glint of jewelry in his symmetrical necktie, stiff derby hat. He was smaller than I, and I felt the uppishness always inspired by outmeasuring a little man. He was polite, modest, simple, without side . . . here was the essence of gentlemanly elegance . . . Winslow Homer might have been taken, as he walked and talked at my side, for a successful stock broker . . .

Metropolitan Museum of Art

LIFE IN CAMP (part 2)

VIEWS of NEW-YORK

UNIVERSITY.

THE NEW YORK UNIVERSITY BUILDING, WASHINGTON SQUARE, c. 1860

Though Homer's story lacks dramatic narrative and is without pace or tension, there are in it major clues to the understanding of Homer as a man and as an artist. Perhaps the significance of some of these facts has been underestimated in the past. First and most important of these is his lack of formal training in art. Homer never had the kind of academic training that almost any young European student would have had. His talent was a natural one and so strong in character that perhaps one could say that he did not need any formal training — he seemed to know by instinct what others had to learn. His parents of course played a most important, if perhaps unplanned, part in his early training by making drawing and painting a familiar household occupation. These factors and his strong native ability as a draftsman with its untrammeled spontaneity made Homer a successful artist almost from the first moment he started to draw. He was obviously born with the eye of an artist, and his instinctive taste was never colored or curbed by the academic conventions of any school. And it was this ability as a natural artist that enabled him at the age of nineteen to enter the lithographic shop as an apprentice so skillful that the owner of the shop could confidently turn over to him some of the more complicated tasks.

Other important clues to understanding Homer and to the appreciation of his art are to be found in his biography by placing special emphasis upon certain aspects of it that previous writers have failed to consider. But by examining these times and events with care it becomes possible to throw an entirely new light on the artist's development, a light that leads to a new understanding and appreciation of the work of one of our greatest artists.

Before embarking for Paris let us examine certain forgotten aspects of Homer's formative years — years that are so crucially important in the life of every artist. To do this, we must sketch in some of the principal features of the "art life" in Boston and in New York, where Homer developed, matured, and tempered his great talents in the 1850's and 1860's before he set out to examine the greater art world of Paris in 1867.

A VOICE FROM THE CLIFFS

CHAPTER THREE

THE ART WORLD OF 1840-70 IN BOSTON AND NEW YORK

"The American is only the continuation of the English genius into new conditions, more or less propitious."

EMERSON — *English Traits*

SINCE THE DAYS of Homer's youth the whole structure of the world of art has been drastically altered, and the traditional ways of thinking about art that would be the guide to any young artist in 1859 are now little more than historical curios. In order to begin to understand the young artist of a hundred years ago it is necessary to remind oneself constantly of these great differences and changes.

The organization of the little art worlds of Boston and New York, when Homer inhabited these provincial bohemias, was relatively simple. In 1859 (when Homer set himself up as a free-lance illustrator) the only public art gallery in Boston was merely a room in the Boston Athenaeum that was used for an annual art exhibition. In New York there was the private gallery of the New York Historical Society, an inaccessible place maintained for the benefit of the members of the society. Other than this were the galleries of the National Academy of Design, where annual exhibitions were held, and in both cities there were a few dealers' shops where pictures could be seen.

So much emphasis has been given in the past fifty years to the strong — perhaps overpowering — French influences on American art from 1870 on that the equally potent British influence that flourished earlier in the century has not yet had its full consideration. However, the fact remains that in the decades of Homer's childhood, youth, and early maturity the principal artistic influences brought to bear upon American artists in general, and on Boston artists in particular, were of British origin.

One of the principal reasons for the decline in British influence in American art and the reason for the rise in the influence of the French school on American painting rests on a most curious and usually forgotten circumstance. The reason why so many young American artists went to study art in France in the post-Civil War period was that British artists did not like to take pupils except at a very high price — the leading painters were earning so much money they didn't want to be bothered with pupils. The school of the Royal Academy was unattractive and poorly run. Whereas French artists — no matter how famous or successful they might be — always considered it their duty (if not a great privilege) to devote part of their time to visiting the studios to criticize the work of young students and to advise them on their work.

Most artists pass through a period in youth when they eagerly receive and absorb all sorts of new ideas. The ideas that are current at this period are therefore of crucial importance because they almost invariably become controlling factors in the artist's life and work. Homer was no exception

to this rule, and for him this period of receptiveness and experiment extends from the time in childhood when he first began to draw and paint under the guidance of his mother down to the time of
his return from Paris. In these years he appears to have been sensitive to all the new ideas current
in the American art world.

Strangely enough the important ideas and influences that were active in America in these years
have not recently been explored with the attention their importance and interest merits. Historians
have frequently been inclined to hurry over this period as a desert of Victorian sentiment to reach
the perhaps more colorful day of Parisian influences of the 1870's. Thus it has been generally forgotten that art in America was, in the period 1840–70, still mainly under the influence of British art.
This was especially true in Boston, where British social standards, British political ideas, and British
literary works exerted a peculiar power among the social and intellectual leaders of the community.
Actually the full force of French art as an important influence on American art was not felt until
some years after the close of the Civil War. By that late date, of course, Homer was a mature man
with his style well developed, his talents well controlled by long practice, and his period of training
well behind him.

As far as art was concerned Boston remained throughout most of the nineteenth century just as
much of a British provincial outpost as it had been in John Smibert's day. Though modern French art
may have found a few friends there, they were not influential until the painter William Morris Hunt
succeeded after his return from Paris in directing the Boston eye and mind in the direction of Millet
and Corot. Hunt devoted his not inconsiderable powers as a social figure as well as his great abilities
as a teacher to the praise and study of "modern" French art, and in the end, after much effort, he
finally succeeded in shaking artistic Boston out of its lethargy until, by 1880, any foggy morning on

Mrs. John S. Ames

TWO GIRLS ON THE BEACH, TYNEMOUTH

SOLDIERS (studies)

Boston Common was said to look remarkably like a painting by Corot — at any rate that was the feeling of all the charming girls in his painting class.

Since Homer stated that before he went to New York he never attended an art school or studied as a pupil under any artist in Boston, it must be assumed that he found other sources of instruction. Most important of these of course was the instruction, received perhaps unconsciously, from his mother at home for she was an accomplished amateur painter. Next in importance would be the prints and drawing books his father brought to him from London. Although he always spoke of his apprenticeship at Bufford's as drudgery, it undoubtedly had the most profound effect upon his development, and its educational value was in all probability much greater than the training offered by any American art school of the time.

But during Homer's youth there were also other powerful influences, which came from abroad to affect the little Boston art world. Perhaps the most important of these were the illustrated British magazines and books then to be found in almost every Boston home.

In the 1850's and 1860's artistic influences in Boston came to it largely at second hand through literary channels or through commercial channels connected with publishing. This fact alone contributed much toward giving Boston art its strong British flavor, and the work of American illustrators of books and magazines was almost wholly based upon the precedents set by British publishers and those who worked for them. British artists not only appealed to Boston art patrons and artists, but were also admired by the powerful Boston publishers and other bookish people who thought of art — if they thought of it at all — as a means for illustrating Walter Scott's novels or other favorite monuments of British literature. When the Boston publishers created a demand for book illustration, they naturally favored the local artists who could produce pictures that closely resembled the work of the leading British illustrators.

Cooper Union Museum

THE WRECK OF THE *IRON CROWN* (study)

Metropolitan Museum of Art

TWO LITTLE GIRLS (drawing)

Metropolitan Museum of Art

FISHERWOMEN

The importance of prints, illustrated magazines, and books as a major influence on the work of American artists of the nineteenth century has often been overlooked, but in the early years of the century almost all young artists gained their knowledge of art from these sources, just as they did in the eighteenth century. The engraving, the mezzotint, the aquatint, the lithograph, and the wood engraving (in the days before the invention of photomechanical processes for printing pictures) were all important to artists, as they furnished examples to copy. The print conveyed instruction in technique. British, French, and American print publishers brought out drawing books filled with all sorts of sketches for young artists to copy. Some of the most famous British painters issued books of this sort — George Morland, John Cotman, Alexander Cozens, to name only a few. These books by their choice of subject pointed out to the student the kind of picturesque details that an artist might draw; the quaint country characters, the children of farm and village, the equally quaint inhabitants of small fishing ports with their distinctive costumes, their boats, nets, sails, anchors — all these things were shown. Then too there were pictures of various ways of rendering trees and foliage, and rocks, the waterfall, the old mill, the ruined tower, cows, sheep, dogs, cats, horses, game birds, deer, pots and pans, and all sorts of gear. These sketchbooks or drawing books had a profound effect upon the work of the young artists who copied them.

The more deeply one explores the manner of thought and way of life of the American artist in the middle of the nineteenth century, the more clearly one realizes how very strange to us today are the feelings, thoughts, and ideals, the perceptions and attitudes of the simple young New England artist of one hundred years ago. When Homer was growing up, the dominant influences in art in Boston remained practically unchanged from the days of Benjamin West and West's many pupils. The memory of most of these men — artists trained in the British school — had somewhat faded and dimmed because in general Boston was not really much interested in her artists. Gilbert Stuart — one of the best of them — had been allowed to starve to death there in 1828, and it was there that Washington Allston's brilliant promise was blighted. Allston was the most famous Boston artist of the time — and he more or less set the tone of the Boston art world, such as it was. Yet even as an old man Allston was not unaware of the new currents stirring in British art — currents that were to be so important in their effect on British as well as on American painting. For instance, in a letter of Allston's written to Thomas Sully in 1833 we find discussed one of the principal innovations in art in the first half of the nineteenth century — the effect of watercolor painting techniques on oil painting. Allston writes:

> Pray have you ever painted a picture from the watercolor sketch of yours which I so much admired? I mean the Mother and Child. If you have not and intend it, will you allow me to advise your copying the watercolor sketch as *closely as possible* as to the colour. I think you will be surprized to find how *transparent* and *silvery* an *exact* imitation of it in oil will be. I am certain that Turner — and perhaps also Calcot [Callcott] owe not a little of their richness of tone to the circumstance of their having commenced as painters in watercolor. The foil of the white paper to which their eyes were accustomed was the secret. To imitate this in oil requires not merely a high *key note*, but a powerful empasto and great clearness of tint. Should you make the experiment, let me caution you against *improving* on the sketch. If you do I venture to predict that your labour will be lost. Try to hit the precise tone, especially in the shadows.*

This idea of copying the color and technique of a watercolor painting in oil colors was one that was destined to have the most profound effect on painting in the nineteenth century. Naturally it gave

*Chamberlain Collection, Rare Book Room, Boston Public Library.

a tremendous impetus and importance to watercolor painting — particularly in England, where the art flourished with a luxuriance unknown in other European art centers. Gradually, after much experiment and no little argument, it changed the basic tone of oil painting from the old golden brown of the old masters to the modern method of direct painting in full color on a white ground. The arguments over the respective merits of the two methods was one of the principal controversies among British artists in the first decades of the century, and the adoption of the silvery watercolor style by the majority of artists marked one of the beginnings of modern art.

In 1836, when Homer was born, Allston was still living, Gilbert Stuart had been dead for only eight years, and though John Copley had been dead for over twenty years, his name and fame were kept alive in Boston by his proud relatives and by his elegant portraits. But for Boston, Allston remained the chief representative of the arts — and it was in his studio that Bostonians saw and heard echoes of the grand London art world. When Washington Allston faded into eternity in 1843, his pictures were already old-fashioned, though the sweetness and charm of his memory lingered in polite circles in Boston for many years. As Allston's light faded, the new light burst upon the horizon, glowing from the prose of John Ruskin's *Modern Painters*.

There may be a symbolic significance in the fact that the year Allston died (1843) also saw the first publication of Ruskin's first two volumes of *Modern Painters*. In Boston the influence of Allston in matters of art was soon replaced by that of Ruskin. It was the writings of Ruskin that turned the attention of our young artists from "the dark sentimental artificialities of Carlo Dolci and Guido Reni" to the study of the grand scientific drama of nature — to the heaving might of the sea, to the

Metropolitan Museum of Art

THE BATHERS (drawing)

terrible grandeur of alpine escarpments trailing with mist — subjects so brilliantly depicted in the works of Turner and so vividly described by Ruskin.

The appeal of the teachings of Ruskin to the New England mind was very strong. It had been pointed out that Ruskin seemed to have so many Boston characteristics that in 1855 he could be considered as practically a native Bostonian, just as Robert Browning and Dante were felt to be honorary citizens of the town. Ruskin's best friend was Charles Eliot Norton of Cambridge, Massachusetts, who in the final decades of the century reigned there as a sort of New England pope of art. His influence as a teacher at Harvard was very great in bringing Ruskin's works and ideas into positions of real power in the American art world. Boston was always accused of considering the plastic arts as mere branches of literature, and Ruskin was read as much for his beautiful word pictures as for anything else. He made art a moral force, and by writing sermons and admonitory tracts about art he made it a suitable subject for discussion among the godly churchgoing public — a vast audience, and one that wielded a tremendous force in American cultural life. Through Ruskin's writings "art" and "taste" became almost theological subjects to be discussed with the utmost solemnity and a seriousness that characterized the highly cultivated circles of earnest Boston and Cambridge folk. His ideas about art were very influential among all sorts of cultivated readers who were not necessarily practicing artists.

One of the reasons for Ruskin's general popularity was the simplicity of his approach to art — it was one that could make every man his own art critic, thus reinforcing a strong natural inclination. Ruskin says:

> Truth may be considered a just criterion in art . . . with respect to the representation of facts it is possible for all . . . to form a right judgment on the respective powers and attainments of an artist. Truth is a bar of comparison at which they may all be examined . . .

Mr. and Mrs. Arturo Peralta-Ramos

WAITING FOR THE BOATS

Mrs. John Pierrepont

SAILING THE DORY

Mr. and Mrs. Arturo Peralta-Ramos

SAILING THE CATBOAT

John Durand, in the biography of his father, the artist Asher B. Durand, describes the powerful influence of Ruskin in America in the 1850's and 1860's in the following words:

> It must be stated here that at this time, the public mind in America had been quickened in relation to art by the writings and teachings of Mr. Ruskin. Whatever may be said of the criticisms of works of art . . . by this eminent writer . . . of his theories, hobbies and idiosyncracies, it is certain that he developed more interest in art in the United States than all other agencies put together. His remarkable word painting, the theological bent of his mind, his ascetic temperament . . . furnished both pulpit and press with material for sermons, news and gossip about art . . . and spread a knowledge of art among people who would not otherwise have given it a thought.

Between the death of Allston in 1843 and the exodus of American artists to Paris after the Civil War there was a period when the strong British traditions in American art had not begun to weaken into a secondary place and the charms of French painting had not quite begun to capture and dominate the imaginations of young American artists. But there was in all Western countries at that time a feeling of rebellious restlessness among the men of the new generation who were eager to shake off the old and to adventure and experiment in new directions. At just this period in England there arose the Pre-Raphaelite Brotherhood — a little group of young painters and poets whose protest against the deadness of British academic painting took the form of an earnest call for a return to nature, to the study of nature, rather than the study of literature, for a return to simplicity and sincerity in art.

Homer came to maturity in 1857, when he was twenty-one years old, and in this year and those immediately following there were held in Boston and New York large exhibitions of modern British art — paintings in oil and watercolor and a few pieces of sculpture. The first show opened in New York in the galleries of the National Academy of Design and it consisted of some two hundred works, a number of them by the leading British painters of the day, including pictures by some of the members of the Pre-Raphaelite Brotherhood. One of the organizers of these exhibitions was William M. Rossetti, the brother of Dante Gabriel, who was the leader of the Pre-Raphaelite movement. Among the painters exhibiting were Holman Hunt and F. Madox Brown. The following year this collection of modern British art was shown at the Boston Athenaeum. At this exhibition there were to be seen a large group — over a hundred — of watercolors, many of them by painters no longer remembered in this country, but among them were examples of the work of Samuel Prout, F. Madox Brown, and Ruskin. He contributed a sketch titled *Study of a Block of Gneiss*, a picture that became one of the star attractions of the exhibitions when by some typographical error it was described in a newspaper review of the show as "A Block of Genius." Perhaps the most noteworthy paintings in oil were Holman Hunt's *Eve of St. Agnes* (the small version painted in 1857); F. Madox Brown's *King Lear* and also his *English Autumn Afternoon*, now considered to be one of the masterpieces of British painting of the mid-Victorian era. Frederick Leighton contributed three paintings, *Pan, Venus and Cupid*, and *Orpheus and Eurydice*.

One of the reasons for the popularity of these exhibitions was that they displayed the work of some of the controversial Pre-Raphaelite artists and also the work of a number of artists who were embodying the teachings of Ruskin in their pictures. American artists and the general public were alike eager to see actual examples of the kind of painting about which they had been reading in *Modern Painters*.

Winslow Homer embarked on his career as an artist just at that moment when the ideas and works of the British Pre-Raphaelite painters were being discussed and exhibited in America. To American

BREEZING UP

AUTUMN

artists Ruskin appeared to be their principal spokesman, and his books and reports of his lectures were closely read and his ideas and teachings were applied to their own work. Ruskin's writings in fact brought about a complete change in the attitude of mind of the artists as well as the public toward art in general.

Though its artists were dominated by British ideas, Boston was not alone in this respect, for the same ideas held sway in New York (and in Philadelphia too, for that matter). At that time one of the strongholds of the British tradition in American art was the National Academy of Design in New York. There the older academicians who ruled the institution held very dim views of modern French art — in the late 1860's and early 1870's they spoke solemnly of "the eclipse of American art." This attitude was not based in any serious aesthetic quarrel; it merely meant that their paintings were not selling. It was a cold economic fact that foreign dealers found it very profitable to sell cheap French and German paintings in New York. The sales of foreign pictures in such a small market naturally cut drastically into the sale of American works.

The New York art world was then at best little more than a pallid transatlantic echo of the London art world, centering around the Royal Academy. In New York the old academicians of the National Academy of Design aspired to the kind of power and prestige enjoyed by the British Academy, with its annual exhibitions and its closely guarded privileges awarded to members. The little academy in New York took a new lease on life in 1865, when after a most successful campaign for funds they were able to open a handsome new Venetian Gothic Ruskinian palace on Twenty-third Street at Fourth Avenue. But in spite of this elegant, modern structure the organization that inhabited it was controlled completely by a tight little group of aging painters.

Mr. and Mrs. James Cox Brady

COTTON PICKERS

The artists who were elected as associates or as academicians of the National Academy of Design in the 1850's and 1860's were all artists of a very conservative stripe — most of them painters working in the safe traditional British manner, or at the very least in the currently popular style of modern British art. It is to be noted that Homer was elected as an associate in 1864 and elevated to academician the following year.

The older artists of New York, brought up on the ideas of Benjamin West and Sir Joshua Reynolds, firmly opposed all influences coming from France, until they were forced to recognize them. The old guard at the National Academy — Kensett, Durand, and Huntington, and a few others — clung to the standards of their youth just as long as they could. Their reluctance to change was one of the main factors in bringing about the organization by a group of younger artists in 1877 of the Society of American Artists when the academy refused to show their Parisian work. It is to be noted that, although a number of older artists joined this group in protest against the academy's inflexibility, Homer was not among them.

Serious-minded younger artists like Homer, imbued with Ruskin's ideas and the high-minded ideals of the Pre-Raphaelite Brotherhood, were naturally not in sympathy with the kind of slick French painting they saw offered for sale in New York by Goupil and Company.

At the time some European art dealers discovered the now-well-known American hankering for imported art. Both French and British dealers established stores in New York, and their agents were busy promoting the virtues and values of foreign paintings while running down the works of American painters. In general the few art dealers in New York were not much interested in pushing the works of American artists. The collectors who bought American paintings were, in mid-century, soon out-

Mr. Edward A. Hauss

A HAPPY FAMILY IN VIRGINIA

numbered by the collectors of French, German, Dutch, and Austrian paintings, which the dealers could buy very cheaply in Europe and sell at a great profit in New York.

In the 1850's in New York there was published a magazine called *The Crayon*, edited by J. W. Stillman, the American Pre-Raphaelite painter, and by John Durand, son of the president of the National Academy of Design. It was through the pages of this periodical that the teachings of Ruskin and the ideals of the Pre-Raphaelites first found wide circulation among American artists.

In 1863 a group of young artists and writers banded together in New York to form the Society for the Advancement of Truth in Art — an organization of Ruskin students led by the English landscape painter Thomas C. Farrer, a follower of the Pre-Raphaelite school. To promulgate their ideas, they founded a magazine, *The New Path,* its pages devoted to serious exposition of Ruskin's ideas and Pre-Raphaelite enthusiasms. Among the contemporary artists whose works were most sympathetically reviewed were the paintings of Winslow Homer, who was highly praised for his truthtelling pictures in the following words:

> Mr. Homer is the first of our artists — excepting Mr. McEntee in his "Virginia" — who has endeavored to tell us any truth about the war. True, he has looked only on the laughing or the sentimental

Detroit Institute of Arts

THE DINNER HORN

side — and yet, the "Home Sweet Home," of the last Academy Exhibition was too manly-natural to be called sentimental — but what he has tried to tell us has been said simply honestly and with such homely truth as would have given his pictures a historical value quite apart from their artistic merit, whatever that might have been. In technical-qualities of painting, if he does not prosper too well, and, in consequence of the nature of his subject, sell his pictures too easily, he may make — doubtless, judging from his excellent beginning, will make — great progress, but he will never paint more real soldiers than these, and those which he sent to the Academy last year. Having shown his metal, what he now needs is patient, untiring study from nature only, with grim determination, or glad, if he can reach so high, let him resist every effort and persuasion to lead him into false ways. Let him shun the "ideal" as he would the plague, and build his right to be ranked one day with the poets, on his knowledge of human nature, and the mastery of his material.

Let those who care to know just the difference between the "ideal" and the "real" treatment, take an illustration close at hand. Mr. Homer's two pictures, Nos. 108 and 144, hang near two of Mr. Guy's, Nos. 102 and 143. Compare the drapery in each; the boys' trowsers with the soldiers'. You see that Mr. Guy is true up to a certain point; he follows nature as long as she is graceful, and does not offend his eye, but, once let her make what strikes him as a discord, and which is a discord, of course, for she, the great poet, makes no music without discords — and, straightway Mr. Guy takes out the offending note, smooths it down, and thinks he has bettered nature's work. Then, look at the landscape in the two pictures; see how vague and unreal are the trees, grass and earth in Mr. Guy's. There is no reason for this, for the strong light on the gate-post shows that the sun is shining clear, but there is nothing else in the picture to tell us so, and although we can see every wrinkle in the boy's face as he distorts it, the foreground weeds and stones, and grasses, nearer to us by four feet, at least, are as dim and pale as if there were a mile of air between us and them. Now, look at Mr. Homer's No. 108, and see how faithfully he has tried to draw and paint the branch of pine against the sky. In ten years he will both draw and paint it better, no doubt, but, insufficient as it is, it is perfectly right in intention now, and has more truth in it, and can give more honest enjoyment than all Mr. Guy's theoretical work. Compare the pictures of these two men, inch by inch; Mr. Homer's you will find signed all over with truth — truth in conception, worked out with faithful striving after truth; Mr. Guy's, you will find — not wholly false, but only true as far as the artist thought would be tolerated. When Mr. Homer can draw and paint as well as Mr. Guy he will . . . paint a great deal better, for he will use the knowledge he will then have gained, not in the service of convention and a false idealism, but in the service of that truth at whose altar he has laid his first immature offerings.

By comparing the actual statement of the aims of the Pre-Raphaelite Brotherhood, as recorded by William Rossetti, with Homer's ideas as expressed in his paintings, and in some of his remarks, it is possible to see how closely he was in sympathy with the stated purpose of the brotherhood. Their guiding rules were summed up by Rossetti as follows:

1. To have genuine ideas to express;
2. To study Nature attentively, so as to know how to express them;
3. To sympathize with what is direct and serious and heartfelt in previous art, to the exclusion of what is conventional and self-parading and learned by rote;
4. and most indispensable of all, to produce thoroughly good pictures . . .

While Homer's ideas coincide almost perfectly with those of the Pre-Raphaelite Brotherhood, in its early stages his work of course never showed much influence of the later, highly mannered work of the Brotherhood and its lesser imitators.

One of the indications of the influence of the Pre-Raphaelite school on Homer is to be found in the faces of the people in his pictures, for it is there that one can plainly see the unmistakable smooth and somewhat vacuous expression so characteristic of the Pre-Raphaelite type. The faces of some of

A LADY (Millais)

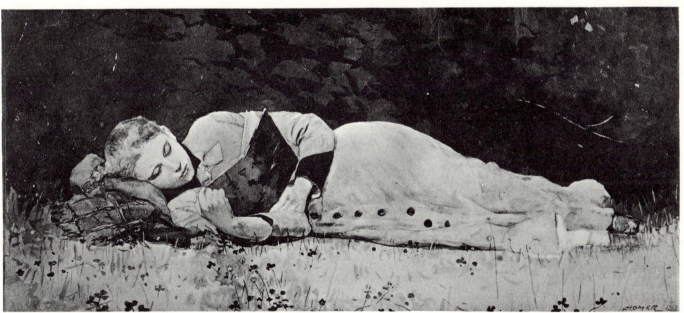

THE NEW NOVEL

the women in Homer's paintings seem to be sisters, country cousins perhaps of some of the ladies of Sir Edward Burne-Jones and Dante Gabriel Rossetti.

Homer's Tynemouth drawings and watercolors, done in 1881–82, show with particular clarity his sympathy with and interest in the style of various artists who were active members of the Pre-Raphaelite group. Two of his best-known works of this period, *Mending the Nets* and *A Voice from the Cliffs*, are plainly drawn in the style of Burne-Jones.

One of the principal features of British art during the period 1840–70 was the absolute predominance of moral and intellectual elements over those that were purely sensory or aesthetic. Subject was then of much greater value than treatment. Ruskin said that the specific painting techniques were the

ILLUSTRATED CATALOGUE

Sixteenth Annual Exhibition

— of the —

AMERICAN

WATER COLOR SOCIETY

HELD AT THE GALLERIES OF THE

National Academy of Design,

COR. TWENTY-THIRD ST. & FOURTH AVE.

OPEN UNTIL FEBRUARY 25TH.

NEW YORK.

1883.

Metropolitan Museum of Art

A VOICE FROM THE CLIFFS

mere language, the upholstery of art, thus dismissing them with contempt. He taught that the visual attractions of a picture were of no significance and that paintings should not be enjoyed for their intrinsic qualities as paintings, but for their truth. To Ruskin a painting was little more than a pictorial sermon. The enjoyment of color, as such, was considered to be bordering on the carnal. Another conspicuous feature of British art at this time was the lack of interest in pure landscape — a form of painting that occupied so many American painters — but in British painting the interest in landscape was transferred to the figures in the landscape.

Metropolitan Museum of Art

SEATED WOMAN (Burne-Jones)

THE BIRD CATCHERS

THE STRAWBERRY BED

WATCHING THE CROWS

ON THE BEACH (Landseer)

THE GLEANER (Millais)

ON THE BEACH AT HASTINGS (Landseer)

These ideas most probably had some influence on Homer — in almost all of his pictures the subject or idea to be expressed is very important to him. He seldom painted landscapes without figures prominently placed in them; many critics found his technique crude; his pictures are never approached with the purely painterly problems in mind that produced the kind of self-conscious preciosity one finds in some of Whistler's work.

In many ways Homer was a typical Boston artist, although we seldom think of him now in just that way. But his frame of mind was carpentered upon a solid foursquare foundation of New England attitudes and ways. Homer's mind was furnished with Cambridge thoughts about art and about nature. And the moral and didactic exhortations of Ruskin made a deep and lasting impression on his mind. They served as a well of inspiration to him throughout his life, and his last great paintings of the sea are almost direct translations, one might say, of Ruskin's prose into paint. It was natural that Homer would find many patrons in Boston — especially for his watercolors — for these patrons recognized in him the sterling New England virtues of a serious-minded home-town boy. They saw in his work the kind of things Bostonians had been trained to look for in a picture. They found in Homer's paintings not only familiar scenes but the safe and sane Ruskin-approved style and subject treated in a straight-forward, truthful way that any solid Boston man could understand without recourse to esoteric aesthetic theories or foreign innovations.

Metropolitan Museum of Art
SWINGING ON A BIRCH TREE

TWO EQUESTRIANS (Millais)

Yet Homer's wider fame and his mature skill were developed in New York. Though he sold many watercolors in Boston, his greatest patron was the New Yorker Thomas B. Clarke. And it was Clarke who finally established Homer in the public mind as a great and desirable artist. In general it was from New York exhibitions and finally from New York dealers that Homer received his greatest rewards in cash, and it was through the writings of New York critics that Homer was brought forcibly to the attention of the American public at the end of the century. His medals were bestowed on him, not by his native Boston, but by artistic strongholds in Philadelphia, and Pittsburgh and by the juries of award at the expositions in Buffalo, St. Louis, and Charleston, South Carolina as well as Paris.

Homer's drawings and paintings in the 1860's and 1870's may be generally characterized as somewhat modified Ruskinian versions of the current style of the best British illustrators. By good fortune at just that time almost all the best British artists were very active as illustrators of magazines and books. Thus their work had the most profound influence on his work. In fact Homer's basic style always remained grounded in the tradition of the British illustrator. This was one of the most important factors in helping him to maintain in his work its unique character, in contrast to the work of most American painters who had abandoned, or had never been subjected to, a study of the solid, simple virtues of the British illustrators. To European critics in later years Homer's work always appeared to be uniquely American, and this was in part because almost every other American artist in the later years of the nineteenth century was trying his best to paint in the currently fashionable French misty Barbizon manner.

Why this obvious — perhaps inevitable — connection between Homer's work and the early work of the Pre-Raphaelites has been consistently overlooked — and it was overlooked by his contemporaries as well as by later students and critics — is difficult to explain. However the modern student of Homer's work will take into account that when Homer came into his greatest fame in the 1890's and in the early years of the twentieth century, all American writers on art were under the influence of some ideas that were then popular. One of these was that all the important influences in modern art had come to America from Paris. Another popular idea was the belief in the importance of the Paris Salon jury as the highest and final authority in matters of art. There was also a general desire to find some purely American painter whose work was conspicuously "national." Thus Homer, because his work was not strongly influenced by the French art of 1880–90, appeared to be pure American especially when his work was contrasted with that of other American artists. In a way the critics were right, for Homer *was* pure American, though not in the chauvinistic manner they believed him to be. He was pure American in that he was carrying on, in his own individual way, the old traditions of English art in New England. And it was there in Boston that he became first aware of the new currents that stirred the London art world in his youth.

Metropolitan Museum of Art

LE CHANT D'AMOUR (Burne-Jones)

Mr. Alfred Corning Clark

HEAD OF A GIRL

A FRENCH FARM

CHAPTER FOUR

HOMER IN PARIS — 1867

"It is not worth while to be alarmed about the influence of French art. It would hardly be mortifying if a Millet or a Delacroix should be developed in Boston."

WILLIAM MORRIS HUNT

IN ONE of the most exhaustive studies of the life and work of Winslow Homer — the book by William Howe Downes — there is an account of Homer's trip to Paris in 1867. This account contains the following statement:

> He did no studying and no serious work of any kind worth mentioning while he was in Paris, and it is probable that he devoted most of his time to sightseeing and recreation . . . What he did not do while he was in France is somewhat significant. He did not enter the atelier of the most renowned French master; he did not make copies of the famous masterpieces in the Louvre; he did not go to Concarneau or to Grez or to any of the favorite painting-grounds of the young American artists; and he did not, as far as is known, make many friends among his fellow artists.

Practically all the other writers on Homer in the past have agreed in general with this incredible statement and they have reiterated the fact that Homer's trip to Paris had no effect on his art.

In the past students of Homer's work have sought in vain for obvious traces of French influence — the mark of some Parisian academy or atelier, or perhaps for the shadow of the manner of some fashionable salon painter of the day. All have decided that since little French influence of this sort is visible in his work his stay in France was without effect on his development as an artist. His wood engraving showing students copying from the old masters in the Long Gallery of the Louvre is taken as positive proof that he actually went to the Louvre, but whether he studied the masterpieces displayed there, or what he thought of them, has always been a part of the enigmatic aspects of his trip.

After some hesitation, in view of the considered opinions of the experts, I wish to propose a new theory that presents an alternative view on this interesting phase of Homer's career. It is my belief that Homer's trip to Paris was the most important event in his entire career as an artist.

Working on the old theory as propounded by Downes, we are asked to believe that a young American artist, a disciple of Ruskin, a practicing draftsman, a professional illustrator and painter, could go from the tame little provincial New York art world of 1867 to stay in Paris for almost a year, and to imagine that this sojourn in the art capital of the Western world had no effect on him as an artist. There was nothing in America to match the glamour and excitement of the Paris art world in those last hectic years of the uneasy reign of Napoleon III. The contrast of American meagerness to the extravagant opulence of Paris in 1867 must have been extraordinary, perhaps even a bit overwhelming, to the innocent American artist's eye.

It would seem most improbable that the man who was to become "the greatest American artist" would be able to spend such a long time in the very center of the art world and yet remain completely blind to and completely unaffected by the exciting new artistic currents of the day, currents that were then pulsing and flowing through the minds and conversations and writings of all the most sensitive critics, the boldest modern painters, most of them young men of just about the same age as Homer. Surely no lively, intelligent young man like Homer, with his keen artist's eye and his active Yankee curiosity, could be so dull, so unperceptive, as not to be aware of what was going on around him. Yet this is what his biographers in the past have asked us to believe.

Before he went to Paris, Homer was the very competent but not especially inspired illustrator who had produced a few paintings worked up from drawings that had been originally made for illustrations. Yet on his return to New York he immediately proceded to work in an entirely new way, and, using this new style, he began to create the unique masterpieces that made him famous.

The pictures of this time are quite different from Homer's work before 1867, and in them his own distinctive style, his bold, characteristic pattern began to emerge. One feels that his hand and eye had been released from the careful Ruskinian search for small truths and trained on something much larger and finer, something much more significant. Beginning in the winter of 1868, Homer's pictures suddenly cease to be mere journalistic illustrations subject to current commercial woodcut conventions. The journalistic report "sketched on the spot" has been subtly transformed into a consciously designed work of art.

What were the important discoveries made in Paris, what were the causes of this marked change of pace, what spurred this advance from ordinary competence to the mastery of a whole new artistic vocabulary? These interesting questions pique the curiosity.

It is not surprising that writers in search of French influence in Homer's work did not find the impress of an academy or an echo of the manner of one of the popular Salon painters. Yet if one studies the paintings Homer actually did in France — such as the landscape painted in the country at Cerney-la-Ville, titled *A French Farm* (now in the collection of the University of Illinois), or his *Girl with Pitchfork* (in the Duncan Phillips Collection in Washington, D.C.), they seem to reflect rather strongly the influence, not of any of the standard gallery gods of the day — Daubigny, Jacques, or Lambinet — but the influence of the rebellious avant garde, especially of Manet.

Another important fact about Homer's stay in Paris, one that has not been noted by his biographers, was the presence there of his old friend the painter J. Foxcroft Cole, who had been an apprentice at Bufford's when Homer was there. When Homer left Bufford's in 1859, Cole also ended his apprenticeship, but he set out to study art in Paris. There he entered the studio of Lambinet, where he worked for three years. After a trip to Italy and a visit to the United States he returned to Paris, and, as his biographer says, ". . . by good fortune fell in with a distinguished party of French painters at Cerney-la-Ville. In 1865 . . . he [Cole] commenced his studies in Jacques' studio in Paris . . . he was on the ground when in 1867 the ripened results of French art were shown in the great Exposition. The glories of Millet, Daubigny, Rousseau and Corot."

Thus it was that when Homer arrived in Paris he found there an old friend whose fluent French and thorough knowledge of the studios and cafés of the Latin Quarter made him an admirable guide. Cole knew all the leading French painters of the time, and through him Homer must have gained a very good idea of what was going on in the French art world. Cole would have been able to explain to Homer the gossip of the studios and the politics of getting a painting into the Salon. For part of his stay in Paris, Homer lived with the Boston painter Albert Kelsey, and a photograph of the two friends inscribed "Damon and Pythias" remains as a record of this happy and fruitful time in Homer's life.

Among the advantages for an independent young American artist visiting Paris for the first time

THE CARNIVAL

RIGHT AND LEFT

CHANNEL BASS

were a number of things he would inevitably be interested in seeing. First of all, of course, would be the exhibition of American paintings in the fine-arts section of the exposition (this appears to have been the first international exposition in Europe that admitted that there was such a thing as American art). Two of Homer's paintings were on display there — *Prisoners from the Front* and *On the Bright Side.* In its review of the exhibition of American paintings the *London Art Journal* singled out these two paintings for particular mention, saying: "Certainly most capital for touch, character and vigour, are a couple of little pictures taken from the recent war, by Mr. Winslow Homer of New York. These works are real: the artist paints what he has seen and known."

Perhaps the next thing a young artist would want to see was the sensational exhibition of fifty paintings by Manet — paintings that had been refused a place in the exposition. At this time Manet was the center of a storm of critical comment, most of it attacking him.

And last but not least, our young artist would want to see the exhibition of Japanese arts and manufactures, one of the great features of the exposition. The fantastic and utterly new beauties of these productions, their strange elegance attracted much attention. The display provided a new stimulus to the already-existing vogue for things Japanese. In the estimation of some of the leading French artists the Japanese prints were a revelation. This exhibition is said to have been the first large public showing of Japanese prints and Japanese arts on the Continent. But Japanese prints had appeared in Paris somewhat before this, and the artists and *cognoscenti* had been collecting and studying them. That Homer saw this exhibition and that he was powerfully affected by it is plainly to be seen in all his subsequent work.

Although almost all writers on Homer have mentioned in passing the probability of some Japanese influences to be found in his work, none of these writers has been aware of the Japanese exhibition in the Paris exposition of 1867. Actually it would have been almost impossible for any young artist in Paris in that year to be unaware of these prints — they were the newest thing, the talk of the ateliers and cafés where writers and artists gathered.

It is surprising to find that with all the interest in European art of the nineteenth century, and with the increasing interest in American art of the same period, the profound influence then of Japanese art on the art of the West has not been very thoroughly explored. Actually, from about 1860 Japanese art was one of the major new influences in Western art, and in its way it was an important element in breaking down the traditions of academies and preparing the way for the modern art movement. The Greco-Roman antiquities so beloved by academies have never really recovered from the blow. Japanese art, especially prints, influenced painters in their manner of working, it changed their way of seeing, it affected their feeling for color and their experiments with composition. It immediately captured the collectors of art and educated their taste in new directions; it immediately found a place in the museums of art and in the teaching collections of art schools that were founded in England and America in the second half of the nineteenth century. Japanese art brought about a revolution in the teaching of the principles of design and helped to re-establish the importance of the designer and handcraftsman at a time when they were in peril of being completely overwhelmed by machine-made atrocities, turned out by the jig saw and steam lathe, the stamping mill, the plaster cast, the thousand and one other mechanical efforts at cheap mass production of "art goods," as they were called. And while the series of international expositions seemed to be principally in celebration of the triumphs of the machine, they also brought to a wide public, beginning with the London exposition of 1862, dazzling displays of Japanese paintings, lacquers, bronzes, enamels, ivories, wood carvings, porcelains, and countless exotic treasures that could be purchased for modest sums.

Curiously enough the Pre-Raphaelite painters seem to have had a strong affinity for oriental art — one of the first collectors of Japanese art and Chinese blue-and-white pottery was Dante Gabriel

Princeton University Art Museum

EASTERN POINT LIGHT

Rossetti. A number of critics have pointed out the "Chinese" characteristics of the paintings of the Pre-Raphaelite school. This term was, of course, first applied as a derogatory judgment before it became fashionable for painters to affect Chinese or Japanese accessories in their pictures. Rossetti had first become enthusiastic about oriental art when he saw the Japanese display at the London exposition.

One of the most important pioneers in the introduction of Japanese art into Europe was Queen Victoria's Minister to Japan, Sir Rutherford Alcock. It was due almost entirely to him, and to his great enthusiasm for Japanese art, that his very large collection was displayed in the London exposition. It was probably at this exhibition that Whistler and Rossetti, as well as the London art dealers, discovered the screen, the fan, and the blue-and-white pottery jar. A few years later Sir Rutherford wrote a series of articles on Japanese art that was published in the *Art Journal* and finally issued in book form in 1878 with the title *Art and Art Industries of Japan*. In the introduction to this volume in some remarks on the London exposition of 1862 he says; ". . . nor was I mistaken in my estimate of the value and importance of such a public display of Japanese industries, fabrics and artistic works. Within a very few years, on my return from Japan a second time, I found Japanese fabrics, silks, embroideries, Japanese lacquer, china, faïence, bronzes and enamels exhibited for sale in the shops of every capitol of Europe. For beauty, grace, and perfection of workmanship, variety of form, and novelty of design, they competed successfully in Paris with the best products of the Parisian ateliers, in Vienna with the Viennese specialties, and at Berlin with the celebrated iron and bronze work of that capital. Superior in taste, design and workmanship, they could be sold at a price far below that of European articles of a similar kind. Since that period continuous and increasing efforts have been made, here and in other countries, to reproduce some of the more characteristic features of Japanese art in designs and colors. If imitation be sincerest flattery, no greater homage could have been paid to an incontestible superiority."

The Japanese collections displayed in London in 1862, in Paris in 1867, and in Vienna in 1873 were sold after the expositions closed, and as a result Sir Rutherford says, ". . . now it is no exaggeration to say that some of the best specimens of Japanese skill and artistic work may be seen in almost every dwelling and collection or museum, where Art in any shape finds discriminating patrons."

The first large exhibition of Japanese art in the United States was shown at the Centennial Exposition in Philadelphia in 1876, and this display was so extraordinary that it not only drew the attention of those who were already interested in the exotic arts of Japan, but it revealed the fascinating beauties of Japanese art to many thousands of people who had little or no conception of the art of any Asiatic country, except, of course, for Chinese pottery and porcelain tablewares, which had been imported in quantities since the end of the eighteenth century.

Mrs. Thomas LaFarge

BY THE SHORE

About this time (1876) Homer made a wash drawing in the style of a Japanese print, showing Miss Japan and Mr. China entertaining Mr. and Mrs. Uncle Sam at tea in a vaguely Japanese interior. The picture is spotted here and there with imitation Japanese seals or inscriptions, as in a Japanese print. .

It would be difficult to say when the first Japanese prints or other works of Japanese art came to Boston or New York, but there is incontrovertible proof that there were some Japanese prints in Philadelphia as early as 1855. Such things might have been shipped to any American port, even in the eighteenth century, when American ships first began making the run around the Horn to Asiatic ports. However, we know that the first Japanese prints that came to the attention of the Boston art world in the middle of the nineteenth century were those in some Japanese picture books that the

Cooper Union

INTERNATIONAL TEA PARTY

architect and painter Edward C. Cabot bought in Boston from a stranded sailor sometime between 1855 and 1860. Doubtless similar things were to be found in New York at about the same time. In Boston these Japanese prints were displayed and discussed by Cabot and his artist friends who gathered in his rooms in the Studio Building. Among these friends were all the progressive young painters of the day — William Morris Hunt, Elihu Vedder, Albion Bicknell, and John La Farge. It is quite possible that Homer was also a member of this group and that he might have first seen the work of Japanese print makers here. According to Hunt's biographer, Cabot's Japanese prints made a perceptible impression on the work of the painters who studied them. Hunt in later years was always telling his pupils, "Study the Japanese!"

One of the first Americans to start collecting Japanese art was Henry Walters of Baltimore, who purchased some Japanese objects in Paris in the early 1860's. But as more and more exhibitions of Japanese art were held and as shops dealing in Japanese art treasures, both antique and modern, were opened in the principal cities of Europe and America, Mr. Walters did not long remain alone in the field.

One of the first Western publications to illustrate in color several Japanese prints was, curiously enough, a report issued by the United States Government in 1856. This was an account of Perry's expedition to Japan in 1852–54. One of these color plates reproduced a landscape print by Hiroshige. As early as 1869 the American art critic James Jackson Jarves published a paper on Hokusai in his book *Art Thoughts*, and in 1876 he published one of the first Western books to be devoted to Japanese Art — *A Glimpse of the Art of Japan*, the first American book on the subject, published at Cambridge.

Metropolitan Museum of Art

AMATEUR MUSICIANS

MENDING THE NETS

GIRL WITH PITCHFORK

SAND DUNE

FISHERFOLK ON THE BEACH AT TYNEMOUTH

In France the man who is generally credited with being the first to bring Japanese prints to the attention of the artists of the generation of 1830 was Felix Bracquemond (1833–1914), who was an etcher and a designer for the Sèvres and Haviland porcelain factories. One story has it that as early as 1856 Bracquemond had "discovered" a little volume of designs and pictures by Hokusai that had been used as packing in a shipment of pottery from Japan. This booklet is said to have been found by the printer Delatre, from him it passed into the hands of the engraver Lavielle, and from him to its "discoverer." Other sources say that Bracquemond had made a collection of Japanese prints before this date, for Japanese prints were supposed to have been seen in Paris before 1856. Perhaps they came to France from Holland, for there had been a Dutch trading connection with Japan in the eighteenth century and collections of Japanese prints were made in Holland at an early date. It is said that there was also a collection of Japanese prints in Sweden in the late eighteenth century. The anonymous British traveler who wrote *Two Journeys to Japan*, published in 1856, is said to have had a collection in England. All these facts rather dim the claims of Bracquemond and the Goncourts of being the "discoverers" of Japanese art, yet they show that Japanese prints were to be found in Europe in several places, waiting for a Bracquemond or a Goncourt to "discover" them and bring them to the attention of collectors who could make them fashionable, and to artists who could find ideas and inspiration in them.

The Paris exposition of 1867 was one of those gestures of government propaganda designed to make the people of France feel that all was serene. It directed their attention away from the very serious political and military situation and brought them the kind of display they loved, a show of pomp and power with fireworks and glittering displays of the royal personages who came to see the show.

Art Institute of Chicago

THE GULF STREAM (watercolor)

THE MORNING BELL

CROQUET SCENE

An amusing glimpse of the French attitude toward the exposition is given in the *Goncourt Journals*. The Goncourt brothers deplored the American influence on France that they detected. They did not realize what was happening or how fortunate it would be in the future — in the very near future — for France to have American friends. It was at this time and in the following decades that the groundwork was laid for French art and French culture to become one of the dominant forces in American art, in painting, in sculpture, and in architecture; also in the world of ideas, no less than in the dazzling world of fashion. In the fifty years from 1860 to 1910 American painters, sculptors, and architects flocked to Paris by the hundreds for training in her art schools, and the ties with France formed then by American students, writers, and tourists, their love for France, for the French people, for Paris, and for French art were factors of the very first importance in bringing Americans to the aid of France at the time of the Franco-Prussian War in 1870 as well as at the time of World War I.

However, in 1867 the Goncourts deplored the Americanization of France just as some of the older American artists at home reciprocated by deploring the growing French influence on American art. The Goncourts wrote:

> The Universal Exposition, the final blow levelled at the past, the Americanization of France, industry lording it over art, the steam thresher displacing the painting — in brief the Federation of Matter.

Yet in another passage the exposition seemed to them dreamlike. They went to the exposition on the evening of May 27 and recorded their impressions:

> Accompanied by Gautier we wandered round that great monster called the Universal Exposition. In this babel of industry we felt as if walking in a dream . . . little by little, things round us began to wear a fantastic look. The sky over the Champs de Mars became filled with the tints of an oriental sky; the outlines of the confused medley of buildings seen against the violet evening sky . . . the domes, the kiosks, the minarets . . . brought into the Parisian night the reflected transparencies of a night in an Asiatic city. At times it seemed to us that were were walking in a picture painted in Japan round an infinite palace, beneath a roof projecting as do the roofs of Buddhist monasteries, lighted up by globes of unpolished glass that gave off the same glow as the paper lanterns at a Japanese celebration.

In another passage they lay claim to having discovered Japanese art and to have made it fashionable. Perhaps this is true as far as the society in which the Goncourts moved was concerned, and perhaps they turned the attention of a few wealthy collectors to the strange beauties of Japanese bric-a-brac, but the artists had found, long before them, in Japanese art, not mere parlor ornaments, but a world of new and exciting pictorial ideas that influenced their work. An entry in the *Goncourt Journals* for 1868 says:

> We were the first to introduce the taste for Chinese and Japanese objects. Who more than we felt, preached and propagated this taste, which has now descended to the middle-classes? Who fell in love with the first Japanese prints and had the courage to buy them?

Note that for the Goncourts the taste for Japanese art was somewhat outmoded in 1868 because it had "descended to the middle-classes"! Note that at first it took "courage" for a French connoisseur to buy a Japanese print!

But perhaps the most amusing and illuminating glimpse of the attitude of French society toward

LOOKING OVER THE CLIFF

Japanese art is revealed in an earlier entry in the *Goncourt Journals*. Under the date September 3, 1865, they record:

> The princess [Mathilde Bonaparte 1820–1904] was terribly revolutionary this evening. With a table full of academic guests to dinner, she asserted roundly and loudly that she much preferred a Japanese vase to an Etruscan [i.e., Greek] vase ...

This of course was before the taste for things Japanese had descended to the middle classes.

The impact of Japanese art on Homer's contemporaries had some very interesting results. Among the artists Whistler became an avid collector of blue-and-white porcelain, he painted Japanese patterns on the frames of his paintings, his famous butterfly signature was not only designed in the Japanese style but it was placed on his pictures with care so it might contribute to the composition just as the signatures and seals and inscriptions are placed on Japanese and Chinese paintings. He stripped his rooms of all Victorian clutter and tried to approximate in his London house the bare, austere, asymmetrical calm of a Japanese interior. This revolutionary style of interior decoration was considered by conventional minds to be quite bewildering. In the exhibition galleries Whistler was the first to use light-colored flat paint on the walls where he arranged his paintings widely spaced in a single line. The effect of such extraordinary restraint in a day of superabundant decoration was perhaps more than bewildering; it was nothing less than shocking. The effect of Japanese art on Whistler was to make him provide a startling background for himself and for his paintings. Other American artists were affected in various ways. Elihu Vedder, for instance, lists among his many "fads" the collection of "Japanese objects and prints, for I am an abject admirer of all things in Japanese art . . ." The impact of Japanese art on John La Farge was so strong it finally sent him to Japan, where he gathered the materials for his book *An Artist's Letters from Japan*.

In later years some conservative French art critics blamed Manet alone for all the corrupting Japanese influences visible in the works of a whole group of younger painters. They complained of the strange compositions — so unlike the Greco-Roman frieze prescribed by the Academy. They said that the large areas of flat color and the simplified modeling gave these new pictures the effect of rough sketches, clumsy and unfinished. Worse still were the unpoetic subjects taken from everyday life — so unrefined, so inartistic. The blame for all this was placed upon Manet, who was accused of advocating this mode of painting since 1860.

Mr. and Mrs. Charles S. Payson

ARTISTS SKETCHING IN THE WHITE MOUNTAINS

A shop dealing with oriental imports — Chinese and Japanese porcelains, costumes, fans, and Japanese prints — was opened in Paris in 1862 — La Porte Chinoise in the Rue de Rivoli. This instantly became a center of interest to artists and art collectors. Practically every studio in Paris was then decorated with a few Japanese paper fans or prints tacked on the wall, and bits of Japanese bric-a-brac. The collectors of Japanese prints soon formed a club where they could compare and dis-

Freer Gallery of Art

VARIATIONS IN FLESH-COLOR AND GREEN: THE BALCONY (Whistler)

play their treasures. The artists' interest in Japanese things, if not in Japanese design, was almost immediately reflected in the paintings of the artists of the younger generation. This kind of influence is seen in Whistler's pictures like *The Golden Screen*, the *Princesse du Pays de Porcelaine*, and in *The Balcony*. In these pictures European ladies in oriental robes toy with Japanese fans and stand in vaguely drooping willowy oriental poses before Japanese screens. In 1868 Manet exhibited his now famous portrait of Émile Zola, which shows in the background a Japanese print and the leaf of a painted screen. At first the taste for the exotic art of Japan was confined to a few collectors and the artists of the advance guard, but it was a taste that spread rapidly and grew steadily in popular favor in the following decades until it came to full flower in the 1890's, when there was a whole exposition devoted exclusively to Japanese art and everyone in Paris and London, New York and Boston was collecting Satsuma jars, enamels, netsuke, inro, brocaded obi, kakemono and ukiyoye prints.

The Japanese print in the 1860's had the same kind of significance for Western artists of that day that the African Negro sculpture had for young artists in the early twentieth century. It was a symbol of freedom from academic convention, a symbol of change, of rebellion, and of renewal. The study of Japanese prints offered to the Western artist of the mid-nineteenth century a refreshing and unjaded point of view, a stimulating new concept of how to design a picture, a totally strange and delightful way of using flat color. The Japanese print offered avenues of escape from the tiresomely familiar refinements of Western art as taught by the academy; an escape from the sacred but dead plaster casts of *Venus de' Medici*, a liberation of the eye from the hackneyed visions of a hundred sentimental Bolognese religious painters, a daring flight from a thousand safe and tidy little Dutch landscapes, an insult direct in the faces of countless battalions of official portraits. To the artists of the 1860's the Japanese print pointed the way to freedom from all this.

It is possible that Homer bought a few Japanese prints or illustrated books at La Porte Chinoise, but he was never a collector of oriental bric-a-brac. His studio was a workroom and it was never decorated to look like the salon of an antiquary, as were so many studios of the time, nor was it consciously planned as a stage for the display of a personality, as was the studio of Whistler. One feels that Homer was content to know about Japanese art without any desire to possess a collection. As far as we know he never "went off the deep end" over blue-and-white porcelains, Japanese robes, or fans, and certainly no one ever caught him posing for his portrait dressed up in a Japanese kimono, as Whistler did.

What Homer took from ukiyoye prints was the strictly practical hints and suggestions directly related to his life work — the designing of pictures. In this he showed most clearly his keenness of perception, his concentration on essentials. Perhaps Homer is at his most Yankee when he chose to keep his mouth shut on the subject of the discoveries made on his trip to Paris. He was willing to leave the porcelains, the prints, the brocades and fans, and the smart art chatter to the shopkeepers, the collectors, the amateurs of art, and to artist-decorators like Whistler.

One feels that Homer's approach to Japanese art was similar to the attitude of Degas, which is so well described in John Rewald's *History of Impressionism*, in which he says:

> Of the Batignolles group, Degas apparently showed the greatest interest in Japanese prints. Their graphic style, their subtle use of line, their decorative qualities, their daring foreshortenings and, above all, the way in which their principal subjects were often placed off-center, the whole composition and organization of space seem to have impressed him deeply. Some of these characteristics were to find an echo in his own works, but, unlike Tissot and Whistler, he did not make any direct use of picturesque Japanese subjects or elements. Quite the contrary, he endeavored to absorb those of the new principles which he could adapt to his own vision and used them, stripped of their fancy oriental character, to enrich his repertory. "From Italy to Spain, from Greece to Japan," he liked to say, "there is not very much difference in technique; everywhere it is a question of summing up life in its essential gestures, and the rest is the business of the artists' eye and hand."

The difference between the Japanese influence on Homer and that on the other American artists of the time — on Whistler or on La Farge — goes a long way toward explaining the differing charac-

Mr. and Mrs. Paul Mellon

MORNING GLORIES

ters of these men and their varying attitudes toward art. While Whistler and La Farge saw and adopted some of the more obvious decorative externalities of oriental art, Homer, like the French painters Manet and Degas, looked beyond this surface of charming quaintness into the underlying artistic principles. This perhaps explains why Homer's paintings now have an interest, an excitement, a vitality, a modernity, that inexorable time has drained out of many of Whistler's paintings; and all these are qualities that were perhaps never very strong in the work of La Farge.

Homer's experience up to 1867 was actually a preparatory period that brought him to the point where he could immediately grasp the value and meaning of Japanese design when it was spread before him. If he had been subject to a long academic training in art, he probably would have been unable to see Japanese prints as anything but quaint little souvenirs of the mysterious East — an attitude that was exactly the reaction of most academic artists when they were confronted with the great art of any Asiatic country; and probably Homer would have been unable also to appreciate the new ideas of Manet that were then enlivening the talk of the studios and cafés. But Homer was not an academic artist — he was independent — and it is evident in his work that the ukiyoye artists spoke to Homer, not in incomprehensible Japanese, but in the universal language of art, of design, of color, of technical mastery. The designer of wood engravings from Boston understood perfectly the message of the designers of wood engravings from Edo, and Homer recognized the Japanese print makers as

Brooklyn Museum

GLASS WINDOWS, BAHAMAS

ADIRONDACK GUIDE

THE FOX HUNT

masters who had something important to teach him about his craft. His sensitive absorption and application of the lessons to be learned from Japanese prints gave his work a significant underlying structure of composition, design, and color relations upon which he was able to create an individual style.

In the late 1870's at least one critic pointed out the influence of Japanese art on Homer's work in a review of the National Academy annual exhibition of 1879. The following significant passage appeared in *Appleton's Art Journal*, and the writer is speaking of Homer's painting *Upland Cotton:*

> . . . a remarkable penetration of Japanese thought into American expression . . . the picture is a superb piece of decoration, with its deep queer colors like the Japanese, dull greens, dim reds, and

Munsion-Williams-Proctor Institute

UPLAND COTTON

strange neutral blues and pinks. Japanese art is not gorgeous . . . but its peculiar and artistic subtlety has been assimilated precisely by Mr. Homer. This picture seems to us original and important as an example of new thought.

In 1935 Allen Weller published an article in *The Magazine of Art* in which he pointed out Homer's St. Valentine's Day illustration, published in *Harper's Weekly*, February 22, 1868, as an indication of the Japanese influence on the artist. Though this print indicates that Homer unquestionably was familiar with at least one Japanese print at this date, in the designing of this picture Japanese art cannot be said to have been much of an influence. Although the author does not connect Homer's trip to Paris with his knowledge of Japanese art he says:

> One of the few definite exterior influences on Homer's artistic development seems to have come from this period however in the form of his interest in Japanese prints. He must have been one of the very earliest western artists to show clearly a familiarity with Japanese art. . . . Later refinements of spacing and proportion perhaps reflect the Japanese influence more subtly and indeed it is to be found in some of his masterpieces of twenty-five years later like *The Fox Hunt.*

Once the idea of Japanese influence on the art of Winslow Homer is accepted, it becomes easy to find evidence of it in all his work after 1867. It was perhaps this as much as anything else that gave his work its disturbing air of extreme modernity in the 1870's, '80's, and '90's. It is probably now one of the main sources of the strength and vitality of his work. One feels that in all justice some credit must go to Hokusai and to Hiroshige, as well as to Ruskin and Manet, for important shares in the development of the distinctive American art of Winslow Homer.

In Homer's case these new influences were always controlled by his early training, influences added to a firm grounding in traditional draftsmanship. He differed in this respect from almost all of the younger artists who went from America to study in Paris in the 1870's and 1880's. Many of them went completely unprepared, with nothing but the most sketchy training in drawing or painting. Very few of them were, as Homer was, already practicing professional illustrators or painters before they were plunged into the bohemian life of the Parisian studios.

Homer was by nature and by training an individualist and a painter of the naturalist school. His self-made success as an artist gave him an independent point of view. Undoubtedly his attitudes and training prepared him to make his own judgments about the art on display in Paris. They predisposed him to profit by the example of Manet and to sympathize with the ideas of the new painters, as expressed by the critics Zola and Castagnary, the defenders of Manet.

The creed of the new generation in France was stated by Castagnary, writing of the Paris Salon of 1863. He said:

> The naturalist school declares that art is the expression of life under all phases and on all levels, and that its sole aim is to reproduce nature by carrying it to its maximum power and intensity; it is truth balanced with science. The naturalist school re-establishes the broken relationship between man and nature. By its two-fold attempt, in the life of the fields, which it is interpreting with so much uncouth force, and in town life, which reserves for it the most beautiful triumphs, the naturalist school tends to embrace all the forms of the visible world. . . . By placing the artist in the center of his time with the mission of reflection, it determines the genuine utility . . . the morality of art.
> Whence does it come? It is the outcome of the very depths of modern rationalism. It springs from our philosophy, which by putting man back into society from which the psychologists have withdrawn him, has made society the principal object of our scrutiny from now on.

GLOUCESTER HARBOR, FISHING FLEET

The same critic writing of the Salon of 1868 says:

Naturalism, which accepts all the realities of the visible world and, at the same time, all ways of understanding these realities is . . . the opposite of a school. Far from laying down a boundary, it suppresses all barriers . . . it liberates . . . it does not bind the painter's personality, but gives it wings. It says to the artist: "Be free!"

Homer's paintings before 1867 are realistic Ruskinian illustrations saved from banality by his naturally independent vision and his uncompromising honesty in seeking and in finding beauty and meaning in the everyday things he knew best. He was obviously not interested in any of the standard "artistic views" or in picturesque Old World subjects. He did not care for the Venetian sunset, the Dutch windmill, the Algerian beggar boy, the Roman ruin — scenes and subjects about which so many of his contemporaries made their platitudinous pastiches.

Homer's concern as an illustrator with the scenes of everyday life was fortified by the teachings of Ruskin, by the example of Japanese pictures, and by the works of the French naturalist school of painting. His attention was by them directed afresh to the life about him at home — to the plain farmers of the Hudson Valley and of New England, and to their sons and daughters working at the homely tasks of the farm; to the life in Negro cabins and cabbage patches in the South — humble scenes that escaped the attention of practically every other American artist of the time; to the simple fishermen and seamen of the New England coast; to the wilderness guides, the trappers and hunters of the backwoods in the Adirondacks and in Canada.

From 1868 to 1910 every drawing and painting produced by Homer shows in some degree the results of profound study and sympathetic understanding of Japanese prints. At first the effects of this study show most clearly in his composition, in the way the human figures are related to each other, and how they are placed in relation to the edges of the rectangle of page or canvas. In his prints the figures become simplified and solid patterns of flat tones, gray and black with white accents, and they stand against quiet backgrounds.

Private Collection, New York

STILL LIFE: WILD DUCKS

WINTER, A SKATING SCENE

It was the study of Japanese prints that gave him the knowledge of how to choose an unconventional point of view from which to look at familiar things, and to look at them with a new vision. It showed him how to transform his skillful reportorial sketches into consciously planned and organized works of art. It makes his wood engravings, designed for Harper's after his return from Paris, stand out in a fine bold way from his earlier work. The new prints, with their strong simple British style, possess a new feeling for harmonious patterning of tones, their unhackneyed compositions, and refreshingly odd choice of subject — all these things, joined with his natural skill, removed immediately and forever all trace of the standard or commonplace vision one sees in the work of the other American illustrators and many American painters of the period.

It would probably be difficult to discover just which Japanese print makers had the greatest influence on Homer's imagination. Probably very few of his pictures can be definitely linked with specific Japanese prints, paintings, or designs. To those familiar with the whole range of Japanese prints Homer's work will only occasionally show borrowed motifs. In fact only once or twice does Homer nod and allow us to catch him stealing some obvious Japanese quainterie, like the Japanese figures in the St. Valentine's Day print, or the curious wash drawing of the international tea party.

But the student of Japanese prints will have no trouble in recognizing the characteristics of the ukiyoye manner, which appears strongly evident in one of the first designs for a wood engraving Homer made for Harper's on his return from Paris. This print was published in *Harper's Weekly*, January 25, 1868. It is titled *Winter — A Skating Scene*. There is of course nothing at all Japanese about the detail or subject of this picture. The new influence is evident only in the general style of composition, the placing and relationship of masses, the flat color pattern, the elimination of unnecessary detail. But perhaps most significant is the feeling that the picture was planned as a whole, and not merely made up of a collection of details. This particular print is not only one of Homer's first pictures designed upon the principles he learned from Japanese prints, but is also one of his first pictures in what is now recognized to be his personal characteristic style.

The next engraving for Harper's Weekly, titled *Saint Valentine's Day,* must have been thrown together in a hurry — it is an obvious potboiler in the old ordinary journalistic illustration style. But the whole lower left quarter of this rather helter-skelter design is occupied by two figures literally copied, line for line, right out of a Japanese print. It is amusing to note, as we examine this picture, that except for the two Japanese all the rest of the figures in the print have a definite 1868 character. Although the idea was to show pairs of lovers from all times and places, the Roman warrior, the Napoleonic dandy, and their ladies look like self-conscious mid-Victorians in rented costumes. But the Japanese, because they were copied directly from Hokusai or Kiyonaga, have an air of genuineness that only accents the obvious fakery of the rest of the design. This is the last print that Homer did in the old common Anglo-American illustrated-newspaper manner; from this time forward he worked in his new style.

One of the benefits of Homer's trip to Paris that has been wholly ignored was his opportunity to study there the works of the modern British painters. The British art exhibition was in fact displayed in the same room in the exposition building with the work of the American painters. One of the principal features of the British display was a large series of modern watercolors shown on racks in the middle of the gallery.

Although he was interested in watercolors before going to Paris (he was, as we have seen, one of the founders of the American Water Color Society), his interest in the medium and his realization of its great potentialities were not really developed until after he had opportunities to study the work of British watercolor artists and oriental art at the exposition. Whether he realized all the subtle connections between the brush of the oriental artist and the brush of the oriental writer would be hard to say. In the 1860's and '70's there was little enough reliable information on Japanese art published in English. Perhaps Homer was familiar with *A Glimpse at the Art of Japan,* by his fellow New Englander, James Jackson Jarves. However, one feels that Homer did not need to read scholarly books on Japanese art, for his perceptive and searching artist's eye evidently told him all he needed to know. Doubtless it was his understanding and sympathetic feeling for Japanese art and the free-flowing brush of the oriental painters that finally did much to release his hand from the restrained British watercolor style and encouraged him to adventure into the pyrotechnic displays of free brushwork one sees in his later watercolor masterpieces.

Perhaps the most subtle effect of the Japanese print masters on Homer's work is to be found in the unconventional use of color that marks both his watercolors and his paintings in oil. This is one of the elements in his work that set him off from his contemporaries in the most conspicuous way. The Japanese sense of color shows plainly in many of his paintings; for instance, the picture of Negro life *The Carnival,* with its rich yet controlled harlequin dapplings of odd tints, is like the kimono design of one of the Eight Famous Beauties of the Green Houses.

The critics speak of Whistler's "Japanese period," but no one ever has applied, or ever will apply, such a term to Homer's work. He did not have a "Japanese period" or a "French period" — his pictures are always Homer's and always American, or at least Anglo-American.

It is not without significance that Homer was of the same generation as the group of artists around Manet, the men who became the great names of the impressionist movement. All of them were in their

SAINT VALENTINE'S DAY

late twenties or early thirties when Homer was in Paris. Manet himself was thirty-four years old, Homer was thirty. They were the men of the new generation — they were the ones who accepted the challenge of Zola's statement:

> The object or person to be painted are pretexts, genius consists in conveying this object or person in a new, more real or greater sense. As for me it is not the tree, the countenance, the scene offered to me which touches me; it is the man I find in the work, the powerful individual who knows how to create, along-side God's world, a personal world which my eyes will no more be able to forget and which they will recognize everywhere.

(Zola, in *Proudhon et Courbet*, 1867.)

Homer's pictures supply all the evidence anyone could need to show, not only that he was aware of the stimulating currents and new ideas that circulated in Parisian studios and cafés in 1867, but how skillfully he could absorb and use them to his own advantage. A long-range view of his pictures shows that his acceptance of new ideas at least stimulated his natural inclinations and played a fundamental part in directing the formation of his distinctive style of painting, a style that enabled him to create a personal world of his own that is always recognized.

By the time he returned from Paris, Homer had absorbed all the basic influences, ideas, and techniques of his art, and the gradual development of these central elements from which his mature style was constructed occupied his attention for the rest of his life. By this time his course was set, and from it he never wavered, pursuing it steadily throughout his life, through adverse criticism, through changes in fashion, and through periods of neglect. He proceeded single-mindedly to his own goal with complete disregard of the cross-currents and variable breezes from Paris that altered the course of almost every other American artist of the time.

Perhaps the banalities of the American art exhibit at the Paris exposition in 1867, when contrasted with the bold naturalistic canvases of Manet, opened Homer's eyes to the direction in which he wished to go as an artist. Perhaps the influence of British watercolors, of Manet and Courbet, and of Japanese art only served to crystallize, to solidify, to orient, vague natural tendencies already present in his work. Perhaps these influences merely served to accelerate his arrival at independent conclusions about art. But, in any case, it seems plain that his stay in Paris supplied him with the time and place for recapitulations, a time for discoveries, a time for choices and decisions, and at this time he made the right decisions and the right choices, which resulted in giving his work the qualities we now recognize immediately as the true American style of Winslow Homer.

FURLING THE JIB

SPRING

CHAPTER FIVE

HOMER'S WORLD: FRIENDS AND STRANGERS, THE GENERATION OF 1830

"All pictures have something ridiculous about them which comes from fashion . . . the less there is in pictures of the transitory element which most often contributes to present-day success, the more they fulfill the conditions of permanence and of greatness . . ."
The JOURNAL OF EUGÈNE DELACROIX, JUNE 25, 1847.

THOUGH HOMER had his friends among the artists of his own generation, he was not, after his first years in New York, very intimate with any of them. Throughout his life he retained his friendship with the Boston boys who had been his fellow apprentices at Bufford's — Joseph Baker and J. Foxcroft Cole. Another friend of his Boston days was the painter Albert Kelsey, who, with Cole, guided Homer around Paris in 1867.

When Homer had first come to New York as a young man in 1859, he had gradually become acquainted with a number of other young artists and book illustrators and he soon found friends among them. When he took a studio in the old New York University Building on Washington Square in 1861, he met a whole group of artists who were installed there as tenants. In 1866, when he was interviewed by Thomas Bailey Aldrich, there were at least nine men with studios in the building. All of these artists except Eastman Johnson are now rather obscure, if not completely forgotten, and their principal interest and value to us here are to provide an atmosphere, a background, a circle of companions for Homer before he withdrew from contacts and friendships in the art world of New York. It is interesting to note that many of these artists who inhabited the New York University Building were men of about the same age as Homer, a good proportion of them were also New Englanders, and a majority of them earned their livings as illustrators of books and magazines.

The University Building seems always to have attracted artist tenants (Samuel Morse had a studio there in the 1830's). There must have been a friendly informality about the place, but most likely artists gathered there because the rents were low and the light was good. But there were also other attractions; the green open space of the park before the building, and the National Academy of Design was then nearby with its school and its annual exhibitions in which all young artists hoped to show their works. The Düsseldorf Gallery was then on Broadway, not far off, and there were in the neighborhood many small foreign restaurants where simple, inexpensive dinners could be bought.

Homer's neighbors and friends listed by Aldrich are a sort of cross section of the New York art world when Homer was first a part of it. It is interesting to note here that Eastman Johnson was, like Homer, a former apprentice to Bufford, the Boston lithographer. The oldest man in the group was Alexander Jackson Davis (1803–92), who was an architect, architectural draftsman, and lithographer.

Davis was one of the leading architects of the time and a prolific artist whose sketches, plans, and elevations are to be found today scattered through the files of almost all the libraries and museums of New York. Two other men of an earlier generation were Cephas G. Thompson (1809–88), a fashionable portrait painter and a collector of old-master drawings, and Edwin White (1818–77), an old-fashioned painter of genre and figure subjects. All the rest of the tenants on the list were of Homer's generation, born in the 1830's. These younger men seem not to have done the kind of work that would win for them the interest of modern critics, and they are really quite obscure. There was Eugene Benson (1839–1908), a portrait painter and art critic who had the good luck to be sent by some generous patrons to Venice in 1873, where he had the pleasure of remaining for the rest of his life. Marcus Waterman (1834–1914) was later noted as a painter of New England landscapes who after many years of living in Boston went to Europe in 1900 and never returned to America. John Augustus Hows (1832–74) was an illustrator and wood engraver noted at the time for his work in *Forest Pictures in the Adirondacks,* a book published in 1865. Two more illustrators complete the list; William J. Hennessy (1839–1917), who illustrated volumes of American poetry; and Alfred Fredericks, a cartoonist, landscape painter, and illustrator of school textbooks.

Perhaps the fact that Homer and Johnson had both been through the mill at Bufford's formed a friendly bond between them, but probably far more important was the natural clannishness of New

Metropolitan Museum of Art

HARVEST SCENE

GLOUCESTER SCHOONERS AND SLOOP

HOUSES OF PARLIAMENT

Mr. William Roerick

EAST HAMPTON, LONG ISLAND

Montclair Art Museum

FISHERMEN ON SHORE

FISHERMEN BEACHING A DORY AT TYNEMOUTH, ENGLAND

THE STORM

Englanders huddling together in the alien atmosphere of New York that brought together under the same roof, Johnson, Benson, Thompson, Waterman, White, and Homer — all Yankees born and bred.

In the spring of 1866 Thomas Bailey Aldrich was interviewing New York artists, gathering materials for his series of articles titled *Among the Studios*. This series was published in the magazine *Our Young Folks,* a quite proper mid-Victorian periodical designed for children. This perhaps made Aldrich dwell too much on some humorous trivialities and on some consciously instructive details for the amusement and edification of his young readers, but if we ignore, in the article about Homer, all the pious padding and one long but almost pointless anecdote about a recalcitrant Negro model, there remains a certain amount of valuable information. Here we have an insight into the life of the artist at the beginning of his career. Aldrich gives us an evocation of the atmosphere of Homer's little studio, and he makes some interesting comments on the work he saw there. In fact Aldrich's critical estimate — and he had to base his judgment on Homer's rather limited output at that time — is remarkably perceptive, considering that it was made by a cub reporter not especially versed in art criticism. Yet he forecasts in his remarks the direction and tone that would be taken by later critics who had the benefit of studying the great paintings that Homer was to produce.

When Aldrich came to interview Homer, he started his account with a long introductory passage describing the building — a gloomy Gothic structure. He writes:

> . . . The University is one of those buildings that have lost their enthusiasm. It is dingy and despondent, and doesn't care. It lifts its machicolated turrets of whity-brown marble above the treetops of Washington Parade-Ground with an air of forlorn indifference . . . it ought to be cheerful . . . the edifice faces a beautiful park, full of fine old trees . . . but it refuses to be merry, looming up there stiff and repellent with the soft spring gales fanning its weather beaten turrets . . . In one of those same turrets, many years ago, a young artist grew very weary of this life. Perhaps his melancholy spirit still pervades the dusty chambers . . . If so, that is what chills us as we pass through the long uncarpeted halls leading to the little nookery tenanted by Mr. Winslow Homer . . . It has taken us some time to reach Mr. Homer's *atelier,* for it is on the third or fourth floor. But the half finished picture on his easel, the two or three crayon sketches on the walls, (military subjects) and the splendid view from his one window, cause us to forget that last long flight of stairs. The studio itself does not demand particular notice. It is remarkable for nothing but its contracted dimensions; it seems altogether too small for a man to have a large idea in . . . It is only a few years since Mr. Homer's name became known to the public. He is the youngest among the men to whom we look for a high order of excellence in the treatment of purely American subjects. Mr. Homer served his apprenticeship as draughtsman for several periodicals, learning to draw before he plunged into colors, as more impatient aspirants usually do. The back numbers of the pictorial weeklies furnish innumerable evidences of his industry and progress.
>
> A better school of instruction could not have been devised for him. Shortly after the beginning of the War, Mr. Homer went to Virginia, and followed for a while the fortunes of the Army of the Potomac, contributing from time to time, spirited war sketches to the pages of a New York illustrated journal. He returned North with a year's experience of camp life and a portfolio of valuable studies. From these studies he has since painted his most successful pictures. Mr. Homer is very skillful in the delineation of Negro characteristics. The engraving which we print on this page, copied by the artist from the original painting entitled "The bright side," seems to us in his best manner. Of course the broad effect of sunlight attained by oil colors cannot be reproduced in a wood-cut . . . The scene is one that was common enough in our camps down south during the war; but the art with which it is painted is not so common . . . We think it was in 1863 that Mr. Homer received his first general recognition as a painter. In that year he contributed to the thirty-eighth annual exhibition of the National Academy of Design two small pictures, which attracted considerable attention, and were at once purchased by a well-known connoisseur. It was our good fortune to be among the many who saw in these paintings, not

UNDERTOW

NORTHEASTER

EIGHT BELLS

only a promise of future excellence, but an excellence accomplished. In an old memorandum book kept in those days, is the following note, which we beg leave to transcribe. "Two little war scenes . . . by Winslow Homer, — his first appearance in any academy. Mr. Homer calls his pictures "The Last Goose at Yorktown," and "Home Sweet Home." The former represents a couple of Union boys cautiously approaching on all fours, an overturned barrel, out of the farther end of which the wary goose is observed making a Banks-like retreat. A neat bit of humor, Mr. Homer.

The second picture shows a Federal camp at suppertime. The band in the distance is supposed to be playing "Home Sweet Home"; in the immediate foreground are two of the boys, one warming the coffee at a camp fire, and the other dreamily watching the operation; but his heart is "over the hills and far away," for the suggestive music of the band has filled his eyes with visions of home. The different sentiments of the two incidents are worked out with gracious skill. The figures are full of character, but a trifle fresh in color, as is also the landscape.

Mr. Homer has greatly improved on his first war pictures, admirable as they were, and has given us several careful works on more peaceful subjects than Zouaves and cavalry charges. Yet we think his transcripts of camp life, the battle field, and the bivouac are the best exponents of his strength. It is to be hoped that his portfolio and his memory will afford him themes for many a noble picture illustrative of the most desperate struggle that the good Knight Freedom ever had with the Prince of Darkness.

T. B. Aldrich

Some of Aldrich's comments on Homer and his work deserve special notice; for instance, when he calls him "the youngest among the men to whom we look for a high order of excellence in the treatment of purely American subjects." Or again, when he speaks of the painting *On the Bright Side*, Aldrich says: ". . . The scene is one that was common enough in our camps down south during the war; but the art with which it is painted is not so common . . ." Although this sketch is quite brief, and though it has other faults from our point of view today, it has its own peculiar virtues in that it provides materials with which to fill in the vague outlines in our portrait of the artist as a young man.

Downes describes a studio party at the old University Building, and it opens up to us a vista into the heart of the rather staid little bohemia Homer shared with his friends there. He writes:

> There were some very jolly evenings in that studio in the sixties. We are afforded a glimpse of the life of Bohemia in a brief description of one of these evenings given to me by one who was there; A dozen artist friends are in the room. In the midst of the hubbub of talk, storytelling, laughter and badinage, Homer himself, sitting on the edge of the model stand, under the gas light, is working furiously on a drawing on the box-wood block which has to be finished by midnight for Harpers. "Here, one of you boys," he shouts, "fill my pipe for me! I'm too busy to stop."

Among the friends of Homer's early New York days were R. M. Shurtleff (1838–1915), the illustrator and landscape painter, and Alfred C. Howland (1838–1909), landscape and genre painter who lived in the same boardinghouse with Homer on East 16th Street. Later when Homer moved into the Studio Building on West 10th Street in 1871, he became acquainted with E. L. Henry (1841–1919) and John F. Weir (1841–1926). In his *Reminiscences*, Weir says of Homer:

> Winslow Homer, E. L. Henry and I, were the three youngest men in the Studios. Homer was then drawing for *Harper's Weekly*, and struggling to get out of it to take up more important work. Our relations were intimate; that is, as much so as one could be really intimate with Homer, for he was of reserved manner. He went with me to West Point [where Weir's family lived] and enjoyed it, even to the pleasure of looking out from his bedroom window over the vegetable garden toward the barn at sunrise; I can recall the tone of his ejaculation — "just look at it!"

These glimpses are especially interesting as they show Homer, not as a solitary old man of the sea, but as a member of a group of busy young men all seeking fame and fortune as artists in the big city.

Early in the 1880's Homer cut himself off almost completely from the New York art world, first by staying in seclusion on the English coast, and then by retiring to permanent residence at Prouts Neck. Here, though he was far from being an eccentric hermit, he was definitely out of the current of the art life in New York. It is said that he seemed to prefer the company of the local lobstermen and fishermen to that of other artists or professional art lovers. Thus he played little part in the social side of the art world after this date and absolutely no part in the politics of the art world. Homer's ambition was solely and simply to be allowed to paint in peace, to produce good pictures, and to sell them for enough money to support his rather modest way of living in Maine. His only luxuries were his camping trips with his brother to hunt and fish in the deep woods; and jaunts to the South in winter with his aging father.

Homer always knew his own worth and he never gave a tinker's damn for the opinions of the world. He never attempted or aspired to become an international social figure like John Singer Sargent, who seemed to take on the characteristic appearance and manner of the Edwardian tycoons he painted. He was not like La Farge, essentially a literary man and an accomplished dilettante in many fields. He made none of the rather elaborate pretensions to being an aesthete and professional wit like Whistler; he never went to Italy, where Elihu Vedder, drugged by the warm charm of Rome,

Worcester Art Museum

THE GALE

THE GOVERNOR'S WIFE, BAHAMAS

dozed away a lifetime pondering the verses of Omar Khayyám. But what Homer did do was to produce some of the most memorable paintings that have ever been made by an American artist.

Today only the names of Whistler and perhaps La Farge are easily recalled among all the American artists born in the 1830's who were Homer's contemporaries. Many of the painters of that generation — even some of the very successful and once-well-known men — have faded into the background, if not into complete oblivion, and their once-great reputations are now remembered only by the students of the history of American painting. However, on occasion the names of some of these painters are still heard; one of these, for instance, is Homer D. Martin (1836–97), who was a friend of Winslow Homer. He is remembered now chiefly as a painter of French landscapes, done in the French impressionist manner of 1880, and for pictures echoing the style of Corot. Another exact contemporary of Homer is the painter and illustrator Elihu Vedder (1836–1923), who painted strange, dreamlike subjects in a bland, vaguely neoclassic style. His pictures are full of odd hints and mildly occult symbolic figures conceived with a rather tame yet carefully cultivated eccentricity. And then there was Alexander Wyant (1836–92), who lost himself in the forest of Barbizon and never quite managed to find his way back into the American landscape. Two marine painters of the time form an especially interesting contrast to Homer; these are the almost completely forgotten Alfred T. Bricher (1837–1908), and the perhaps better-remembered William T. Richards (1833–1905). Bricher painted scenes along the New England shore where green meadows slope to placid bays and backwaters, but never attempted to represent the more formidable aspects of the sea. W. T. Richards was famous in his day

SHIPBUILDING, GLOUCESTER

for his minutely finished oils and watercolors of surf and rocks, views of the shoals and rocky isles around his Newport studio, as well as more dramatic marine views of the English Channel.

This of course does not exhaust the list by any means, for there are many more of Homer's contemporaries yet unmentioned; for instance, there was J. G. Brown (1831–1913), the painter of ragamuffins, newsboys and bootblacks; and William Gedney Bunce (1840–1916), whose vision was permanently warped by his first sight of Venice; and Samuel Colman (1832–1920), first president of the American Water Color Society; and Charlotte Coman (1833–1924) famous in her day for her skill in painting landscapes in the silvery-gray manner of Corot; and Edward Gay (1837–1928), also a landscape painter; and William S. Haseltine (1835–1910), the Philadelphia artist who lived so long in Rome he might really be considered an Italian painter. Other men of this generation whose memory still lingers with us are Thomas Hovenden (1840–95), whose fame rests almost entirely on his two paintings *The Last Moments of John Brown* and *Breaking Home Ties*; and William Keith (1839–1911), the painter of California landscapes; and Thomas Moran (1837–1926), whose vast slick canvases of Western scenic monuments were popular fifty years ago. There are of course many other artists who could be mentioned, but these perhaps will suffice as a background of contemporary American painters.

The works of most of these artists form a marked contrast to that of Homer, and in reviewing their paintings in relation to his one is struck by the way in which this comparison brings forth in a very clear light the principal qualities that separate him from his contemporaries. These qualities, it will be seen, are the ones that have played such an important part in winning for Homer the assured regard of posterity. First of these characteristics is their sentimentality and his lack of it; there is also in their work, even in some of the very best, a certain provincial note of timidity and vacillation in contrast to Homer's direct unself-conscious boldness; and again, in their work one finds a tame, derivative French conventionality, as opposed to his serenely obtuse Anglo-Yankee independence.

By contrasting Homer with some of his contemporaries it is possible to see to just what degree they scatter their abilities while Homer is always concentrating his on the making of pictures. It is impossible to imagine Homer as anything but a maker of pictures, but his contemporaries Whistler, La Farge, Vedder, Hunt were all various men with several careers as authors, teachers, designers of stained glass, decorators; they were men of many talents, talents they diffused and divided among multiple interests, whereas Homer's powers were always concentrated on the essentials of his life

Cincinnati Art Museum

SUNDAY MORNING IN VIRGINIA

work — drawing, painting, and the designing of pictures. He did not dissipate his genius by writing books, giving lectures, teaching young ladies to draw, designing furniture, or planning interior decorations. He did not waste his time with lawsuits and public quarrels, as did Whistler. Although Whistler painted some pictures and etched a number of plates, he was always at heart an actor. La Farge was a writer and craftsman, an art critic and a decorator. Vedder was a loquacious storyteller and plodding poet who dabbled in all the arts from sculpture to poker-work; his book *The Digressions of V* is a mine of information, a fascinating and irritating welter of veiled hints that are never explained or resolved. Whistler and La Farge were influential in their time as interior decorators — perhaps they were among the first men of their class to enter this field formerly occupied exclusively by professional upholsterers. Hunt was a molder of opinion who introduced the art of Millet and of Barye to the collectors of Boston, and in general to the art lovers of the United States. But all of these men also painted pictures.

There is an urgency of creative power evident in almost every drawing or painting that Homer made, an urgency one feels must be another of the significant qualities that set his work apart from that of his American contemporaries. The facility and drive that animate his work are qualities that can scarcely be discovered in the paintings of Whistler. Nor is this important enlivening quality to be found in the works of La Farge, for his work, accomplished as some of it may be, always retains the tentative mark of the dilettante. Since La Farge never overcame this fault, his paintings never rise to the same professional degree of mastery that is evident in all of Homer's paintings. This same criticism may also apply to the work of William Morris Hunt, whose best work was done in the role of a teacher who opened the eyes and minds of a whole generation of Bostonians to the world of French art. Yet as a painter Hunt's work was derivative and Parisian. Although Homer produced some juvenile humorous sketches during the Civil War, he soon passed beyond this phase to more mature matters. He never became stalled in the rather sophomoric pseudomysticism and conscious quaintness of Elihu Vedder, nor did he fall into using that deadly pyrographic style that mars so many of Vedder's illustrations.

Of all the American artists who were exact or near contemporaries of Homer only Whistler now retains any wide renown. Homer and Whistler were the two leading American painters of their generation, and it would be difficult, perhaps impossible, to discover two more widely differing personalities. Indeed these two artists present in their lives as well as in their pictures the most extreme contrast. At base they were diametrically opposed, both as men and as artists. Whistler always considered himself as the most amusing and melodramatic spectacle, he deliberately sought notoriety, he considered the adulation of his little group of admirers as a fitting tribute to his genius and allowed them to call him "Master." He was fantastically vain of his appearance and his reputation for wit. One feels in fact that Whistler's paintings were really only a part of the theatrical setting he created for himself, an exotic background before which he paraded himself in the elegant and slightly eccentric costumes he affected. His paintings were hardly more than accessories to his pose as a genius. Of course the question may be raised as to whether Whistler was an American painter or merely a pseudo-British aesthete of the yellow nineties. As children one imagines Homer as a sort of Tom Sawyer type with a pocket full of toads and string, but Whistler one sees in imagination, as a little Lord Fauntleroy existing on the cold fringes of the imperial Russian court at St. Petersburg, dressed in black velvet and lace, standing in the formidable shadow of Mother.

Today Whistler seems like an antique, a shadow lingering in the dim, artistic nineties. His paintings are, with few exceptions, also fading into the shadows; they now seem to be mere vaporous wisps, artistic wraiths redolent of a kind of aestheticism that is now feeble and outmoded. His pictures seem devitalized; what was considered in them to be an expression of the highest degree of artistic suggestion seems now to look more like serious technical ineptitude. This is especially apparent in his portraits, for they now display the shakiness of his draftsmanship and the monotony of his color and compositions. Whistler never could make a figure stand up on its own feet; the subtle architecture of the human foot always eluded him. His artistic triumphs were, one feels, the unplanned, accidental successes of the inspired amateur rather than the consciously designed and confidently executed performances of professional mastery. Some of his pictures have blackened and crackled beyond the repair of modern restoration techniques. The evanescent charm of many of his etchings has evaporated, leaving only a residue of scratchy lines into which it is almost impossible to read any significance.

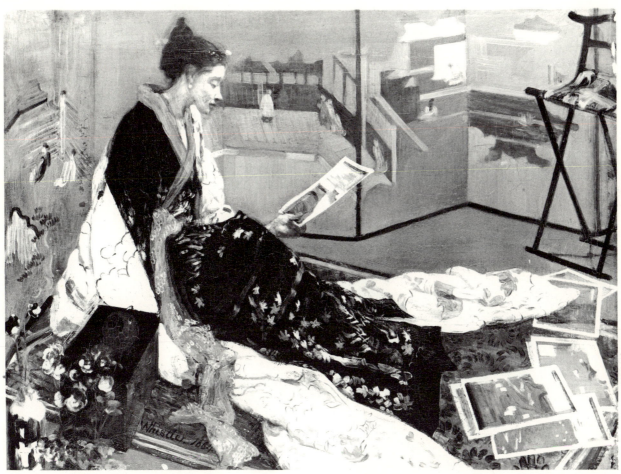

Freer Gallery of Art, Smithsonion Institution, Washington, D.C.

CAPRICE IN PURPLE AND GOLD: THE GOLDEN SCREEN (Whistler)

Whistler was "artistic" to a degree, but he was not in the last analysis an artist. He claimed the rewards of an artist without being able to pay for them in solid coin honestly earned by work and self-discipline.

One very interesting aspect of the contrast between Homer and Whistler is shown by the amount and kind of material published about them. Perhaps a half-dozen books about Homer have been published, perhaps a hundred, maybe two hundred or more articles and essays about him have appeared in magazines, there are perhaps a dozen exhibition catalogues devoted to his work — much more material to be sure than there is about most American painters of the nineteenth century. Yet when this array is compared to the published material about Whistler, it shrinks to almost nothing. There are whole shelves of books written about Whistler; he was in fact the author of some works about himself. His literary friends and his own activities as a writer have won him a position as a *fin de siècle* literary figure, and he begins to loom in cultural histories as an important British bohemian, while his importance as an American painter has steadily decreased.

Homer remains today as a significant and vital American artist, a man whose personal vanity is expressed only in his self-effacement. Whistler's vanity is expressed freely in everything he did and said and it is expressed so persistently it ends by becoming a bore. Although he slashed about him with his sharp wit and occasionally made some really telling — perhaps wounding — remark, much of his recorded conversation now rings with a petulant juvenile note and his writings have an unpleasant air of cheap vindictiveness. His play of wit, so famous in its day, seems to have been not much more than an exchange of trivial quips with Oscar Wilde. Unfortunately Whistler's smart attitude is reflected in his pictures, and it perhaps contributed to their shallow appearance; they are too often mincingly clever and self-consciously "artistic."

One of the most marked contrasts between Homer and Whistler lies in their influence upon their contemporaries, their friends, and followers. Homer's influence was never very great, and what there was seems to have been quite indirect, for he had no pupils, he was not the leader of a group of artists. He is said to have influenced the work of several younger men among the illustrators

Art Institute of Chicago

FLAMBOROUGH HEAD, ENGLAND

WAITING FOR A BITE

in the 1870's. Undoubtedly his work helped to arouse a new enthusiasm for watercolors. Certainly his success turned the attention of several younger painters to the possibilities of marine views. But most important of all, it was due in no small part to Homer's work that Americans were continuously reminded that scenes of everyday life in America were just as valid subjects for the artist as any Thames-side or Venetian view. And this fact was one that many artists and art lovers in the 1880's and '90's were prone to overlook. In those days most American painters were bent on being little Frenchmen and they pulled wires and strove mightily to get their pictures exhibited in the Salon in Paris, for that was thought to be the correct way to assure a sale for their paintings in America. Homer also had a certain amount of influence among the collectors who bought his work, for many of them were themselves in a position to be influential in setting trends in taste. Most notable among these were the collector-dealer Thomas B. Clarke in New York and Edward Hooper of Boston, the latter a trustee of the Boston Museum of Fine Arts as well as the treasurer of Harvard College.

Homer's influence was solely through his work; it never was the result of his personal exertion or his social position. He was never an *arbiter elegantiarum.* On the other hand Whistler exerted a great influence on art in his time and after. Yet it seems that the teachings of Whistler rapidly degenerated from the high goals at which he may have been aiming, and in the hands of his followers these aims fell short of the mark, to a much lower level of pallid and unhealthy aestheticism. There they seemed to flower in a clammy and vaporous atmosphere of art chat, an atmosphere where artistic old ladies at tea parties were heard worshiping "The Master" and "art for art." But the beliefs of these followers of

Whistler were soon to be scattered and swept away in the cold tornado of modern art.

Yet in spite of their vast differences, surprisingly enough, these two artists still can be found to have at least some important things in common. They both lacked the traditional kind of training that European artists in the nineteenth century were supposed to have. In a sense they were both self-taught, but while Homer worked at his lessons Whistler only dreamed about them. When Whistler went to Paris to study art, he was notoriously casual about doing any real work — he preferred the cafés, he read Murger's *Scènes de la vie de Bohème*, but scarcely troubled to appear in the atelier, and what he learned he appears to have learned at third hand from other students. One feels that as an artist Whistler never could have survived anything like Homer's apprenticeship in a commercial lithographer's shop in cold Boston, nor could he have applied himself to earning his own living by turning out illustrations for *Harper's Weekly*. Whistler was altogether too lazy to discipline his talent, and his specious airs of aristocratic superiority blinded him to the plain value of work.

Homer's way was always the hard, objective way of professional competence and personal independence. Whistler's way was the soft, subjective way of the aristocratic dreamer in conflict with the gross Philistine world beneath him. Homer never cultivated a public personality; as a person, in spite of biographers, he scarcely exists apart from his work. He hides behind his pictures and we catch only fleeting glimpses of the man flickering through a pointed phrase in a letter or reported in the conversations of others. Homer felt that his life was a private affair, and as we have seen, he did everything he could to keep it that way. His work completely overshadows the dimly seen person of the painter. Conversely, Whistler's work is almost completely overwhelmed by the flamboyantly artistic personality of Whistler.

Mr. and Mrs. Paul Mellon

YACHTING GIRL

LUMBERING IN WINTER

In opposing Homer and Whistler, Kenyon Cox (in his essay on Homer) indicates where the contrasts lie between "the brilliant cosmopolitan" and "the recluse of Prout's Neck; between the dainty symphonist whose art is American only because it is not quite English and not quite French, and the sturdy realist who has given us the most purely native work, and it is perhaps the most powerful yet produced in America." And today we see that the brilliance of Whistler is time-dimmed and faded, and the "dainty symphonist" now appears in history not primarily as a painter but as a *boulevardier* of the 1890's — a public character — not quite an artist, not quite an author, not quite an actor, but partaking of a little bit of all of these roles, just as he was not quite English, and not quite French, and not quite American.

To contrast the work of these two men reveals that Homer's pictures, while not exactly modern, are marked by a resilient and lively aspect that attracts and holds the attention of the modern observer. These pictures have not aged so much as they have mellowed, and somehow they have escaped from becoming "period" antiques. Yet the passage of time seems inexorably to drain the lifeblood out of Whistler's work even while it seems to enhance the work of Homer.

Homer's ideas about painting were seldom expressed for publication. Perhaps the only remarks of this sort that were published during his lifetime appeared in Sheldon's *Hours with Art and Artists*. Sheldon records the following remarks:

Of Bouguereau . . . Mr. Homer says: "I wouldn't go across the street to see a Bouguereau. His pictures look false; he does not get the truth of that which he wishes to represent; his light is not out-door light; his works are waxy and artificial. They are extremely near being frauds. I prefer every time . . . a picture composed and painted out-doors. The thing is done without your knowing it. Very much of the work now done in studios should be done in the open air. This making studies and then taking them home to use them is only half right. You get composition, but you lose freshness; you miss the subtle and, to the arist, the finer characteristics of the scene itself. I tell you it is impossible to paint an out-door figure in studio-light with any degree of certainty. Out-doors you have the sky overhead giving one light; then the reflected light from whatever reflects; then the direct light of the sun; so that, in the blending and suffusing of these several luminations, there is no such thing as a line to be seen anywhere. I can tell in a second if an out-door picture with figures has been painted in a studio. When there is any sunlight in it, the shadows are not sharp enough; and, when it is an overcast day, the shadows are too positive. Yet you see these faults constantly in pictures in the exhibitions, and you know that they are bad. Nor can they be avoided when such work is done indoors. By the nature of the case the light in a studio must be emphasized at some point or part of the figure; the very fact that there are walls around the painter which shut out the sky shows this. I couldn't even copy in a studio a picture made out-doors; I shouldn't know where the colors came from, nor how to reproduce them. I couldn't possibly do it. Yet an attempted copy might be more satisfactory to the public, because more like a made picture."

Homer was at heart a searcher for truth — the hard truth of life unadorned with poetic beauties, the plain truth, simple and often rather stark. But Whistler, on the other hand, sought not Ruskinian truth to nature; he sought the fleeting illusion of beauty, fragile, evanescent and dreamlike, illusions so fugitive they can exist only in a specially created atmosphere.

And the special atmosphere Whistler created for his pictures no longer exists — his pictures suffer for the lack of it. Yet the truth of Homer's pictures remains today the same truth, and while Whistler's pictures languish in aesthetic backwaters, Homer's pictures continue to speak to us in clear, living accents.

Today their positions are reversed — an exhibition of paintings by Homer is an event of general

THE BEACH AT LONG BRANCH

interest, but the exhibition of Whistler's most famous painting — the portrait of his mother — has been met in recent years with an indifference that borders on the absolute.

If there are strong contrasts and curious parallels between Homer and his American contemporaries, these contrasts become stranger and stronger when he is compared to his contemporaries among European artists. The French painter Fantin-Latour and the German Franz von Lenbach were both exact contemporaries, and among his near contemporaries were three of the great French masters of the nineteenth century — Degas, Manet, and Cézanne, as well as the popular illustrator Gustave Doré, and the British designer William Morris.

Though Homer was no mean draftsman, he cannot compete on equal terms with Degas, who was one of the greatest draftsmen who ever lived; as a painter Homer produced work that was never so fluent or so rich as that of Manet; Homer had no influence comparable to that of Cézanne; as an illustrator Homer cannot be compared to prolific and facile Doré, who turned out pictures by the thousands. Yet Homer's work speaks to Americans in a familiar accent that no amount of French finish or facility can supplant, and we accept him with his faults because they are perhaps our faults and because he belongs to us.

Up to this point we have considered Homer in relation — usually in contrast — to the artists of his time, and though these contrasts show us various aspects of Homer the artist, there are other aspects to the man. Perhaps merely to name a few artists sharpens our perceptions of his individuality when he is compared or contrasted with them, yet merely to place him against the background of his fellow artists gives only a partial picture, for the artist must always be considered also as a part of life in general, not just as an inhabitant of the confines of the art world.

For instance, Homer's life spans the days of Lincoln and John Wilkes Booth through the lean and fat years that the historians now call the "Great Barbecue" or the "Gilded Age" the time of the robber

Metropolitan Museum of Art

TWO LADIES

barons, of trusts and trust busters, the days of General Grant and Ward McAllister, of Mrs. Astor and Henry Ward Beecher and Theodore Roosevelt and down to the eve of World War I.

If, as we are told, the artist reflects in his work aspects of the dominant thought of his time, it may be rewarding to attempt to trace in Homer's work, if we can, the reflection of some of these ideas. As a beginning in this direction perhaps a brief list of the prominent men and women who were his contemporaries (those born in the period 1830–40) will furnish clues; but in any case these names create, merely by their recital, a cultural and historical background from which the formal biography and the critical art essay have perhaps too well isolated him. The names of these people have the power to recall a whole era, and when Homer is placed among the active and influential men and women of his generation whose life work lay in fields not closely associated with art, it widens our understanding of the painter and shows us the man as a part of the society that nurtured and supported him.

There are of course countless thousands who might be mentioned, but certain key names stand out among notable Americans of that time. For instance, in the field of politics and power the Civil War heroes immediately come to mind — Lincoln, Grant, and Lee; in the sphere of business and finance would be the elder J. P. Morgan, Andrew Carnegie, John D. Rockefeller, Hetty Green, Jay Cooke, Jay Gould, Cornelius Vanderbilt, and John Jacob Astor. Among the grand merchant

CHILDREN PLAYING UNDER A GLOUCESTER WHARF

THE GREEN DORY

princes of the time Benjamin Altman, Marshall Field, and A. T. Stewart were the leaders. In the literary world Homer's contemporaries include writers as various as Henry Adams, Emily Dickinson, Mark Twain, William Dean Howells, Bret Harte, Louisa M. Alcott, and Horatio Alger. Among the great naturalists of the period would be John Muir and John Burroughs. Among the legal lights Joseph Choate and Elihu Root. Among Europeans one might mention Lewis Carroll, George Du Maurier, Jules de Goncourt, Christina Rossetti, Johannes Brahms, Émile Zola, Peter Tchaikovsky, and Krafft-Ebing.

In listing these names it is not to suggest that Homer had any personal contact with any of them, yet because of his dominant position in the American art world of that period he must exist in the same milieu in which all these disparate characters operate. They form with him an atmosphere of time and place.

Does Homer's work reflect the renewed interest in the preservation of the wilderness advocated by John Muir; does it reflect the deep interest in the creatures of the forest and field that one finds in the works of John Burroughs? Or is his interest in the wilderness nothing more than a reflection of the pioneer spirit of despoiling and exploiting the natural resources of the land without thought of its consequences? Is Homer's preoccupation in later years with the brute forces of waves and rocks a reflection of the general preoccupation of American leaders with their brutal struggle for power? Or can we say that Homer's interest in the deserted Maine coast in winter, in the Canadian or Adirondack wilderness, in the Caribbean frontier of primitive islands reflect the effort of the sensitive man to escape from all these intellectual forces, or ideas, or blind urges that formed the mentality of the period; an effort to escape from all social responsibilities into the safe dream world of the artist?

Photograph from William Howe Downes

HOMER IN HIS STUDIO AT PROUTS NECK

THE PIONEER

HUNTER IN THE ADIRONDACKS

SNAP THE WHIP

CHAPTER SIX

HOMER AS ILLUSTRATOR
OF BOOKS AND MAGAZINES, 1859-75

"The busy scene depicted . . . by our artist, Mr. Homer, is a faithful
representation, sketched for us from life . . ."
Ballou's Pictorial Drawing-Room Companion, 1857.

WINSLOW HOMER must have been one of the very few important American artists who served an
apprenticeship in a lithographer's shop in the old-fashioned way and then went on to become a
free-lance illustrator while establishing a reputation as a painter. In its way Bufford's Boston lithography shop and printing establishment were Homer's Academy of Fine Arts; the annual shows at the
Boston Athenaeum were for him Louvre and Salon; and in the early days the editors of *Ballou's*
Pictorial and *Harper's Weekly* were the vitally important patrons who enabled him to approach his
goal of financial and artistic independence.

Homer had the good fortune to end his apprenticeship at Bufford's just at the time when the new
and flourishing pictorial periodicals created a demand for illustrators. In fact Homer's work as an
illustrator coincides almost exactly with the period in which magazine publishers were most eager to
employ artists. When Homer ceased to make and sell illustrations in the later 1870's, the newly
invented mechanical processes for reproducing photographs were just about to put an end to the wide
employment of artists as illustrators. By that time Homer was able to pursue his independent way
by the often-precarious but continuing sale of his watercolors and oil paintings.

Homer's work as an illustrator has always been called a prelude to his greater work as a painter.
The years he devoted mainly to illustration were indeed a time of training for his hand and eye — a
training that had the greatest effect upon his pictures. His practice as an illustrator undoubtedly
brought under firm control his ability to draw quickly and easily. With maturity this practice and
control gave him the flashing dexterity he was able later to display in his watercolors.

Much has been made of the distinction between Homer's work as an illustrator and as a painter.
However, this distinction is really rather an arbitrary one. His illustrations and his paintings are
frequently related, and many of his pencil sketches were worked up first into salable illustrations,
then at leisure developed into watercolors and further elaborated into oil paintings, and a few of
these are even carried another step to become etchings. Thus one pictorial idea becomes salable in
various forms, for Homer was not the man to let any of his work go to waste.

The Civil War provided the young illustrator with a whole new range of subjects, and from these
he drew the ideas embodied in his first really important painting — *Prisoners from the Front* — a
painting that placed him in the front rank of the younger artists when it was shown at the National
Academy of Design's annual exhibition in 1866. But, important as this success may have been in the

life of the artist, the changes brought about by the war had other equally important effects on him. His work as "artist correspondent" for *Harper's Weekly* took him into new places and exposed him to new circumstances quite different from the placid round to which he had been accustomed in Boston. The war and other events of the time lifted him out of the safe, familiar New England background of his boyhood and youth and sent him to make for himself a place in the fantastic metropolis of New York, they sent him to Washington and farther south to Virginia on the Peninsular Campaign, and all these strange experiences brought him their reward in the rapidly developing maturity to be found in his work.

During the war Homer made three series of lithographs illustrating the trials and rough humors of life in an army encampment. These pictures, though they cannot claim any very imposing place in his work, still have a certain amount of interest as historical documents, if not as important works of art. The best-known series is the set of seven or eight large lithographs called *Campaign Sketches*. These were issued by L. Prang of Boston about 1864 with a handsomely decorated title page. The subjects shown are similar to the Civil War subjects drawn for *Harper's Weekly*, and their titles reveal the character of the set: *Our Jolly Cook*; *Soldiers Playing Cards*; *The Letter Home*; *A Pass-Time*; *The Baggage Train*; *Foraging*; and *Coffee Call*. The complete set with its decorated cover is now an excessively rare item not to be found in many print collections and seldom seen on the market. The Avery Collection of the New York Public Library has proofs of three of these prints and a proof of the title page with the word "Campaign" misspelled "Campagne."

The other Homer lithographs of the Civil War are two little sets of so-called "cigarette cards." These were also issued by Prang of Boston with the title *Life in Camp*. Each set consists of twelve cards. The titles in set No. 1 are: *Building Castles*; *Hard Tack*; *Upset His Coffee*; *Water Call*; *A Shell is Coming*; *Riding on a Rail*; *Surgeon's Call*; *An Unwelcome Visit*; *Late for Roll Call*; *Stuck in the*

Butler Institute of American Art

SNAP THE WHIP

CAMPAIGN SKETCHES (uncorrected proof of title page)

THE LETTER HOME, FROM CAMPAIGN SKETCHES

Mud; The Guard House; Tossing in a Blanket; the second set contains the following titles: *In the Trenches; Good Bye; Fording; Extra Ration; The Field Barber; The Girl He Left Behind Him; Drummer; A Deserter; Home on a Furlough; The Rifle Pit; Teamster;* and *Our Special.*

The most interesting of all these is the one called *Our Special,* for it is a self-portrait, a caricature of the artist seated on a cannon, making a sketch.

Homer's complete work as an illustrator is really not very extensive. His illustrations appear in only about two dozen books, and in all he produced only about two hundred pictures for the illustrated magazines, *Harper's Weekly, Ballou's Pictorial, Appleton's Journal,* and a few other less-well-known periodicals. It seems clear that he always aspired to be a painter and that his work as an illustrator was merely a convenient means of earning a living while studying painting and establishing himself as an artist. He was not one of those natural-born illustrators like Gustave Doré, who could adapt himself to any text and turn out pictures by the thousands. In fact some of Homer's least effective work is to be found among his illustrations of news events and his illustrations for magazine fiction. As Professor Mather says: "Homer's work for the magazines was rarely illustration in any true sense, but rather graphic reporting or pure picture-making for there was no text to be considered."

As an artist Homer was always so independent, so self-centered he never was eager to work in subordination to an author. Even in his work as a reporter of news events there is plain evidence that work of this sort never won his deeper interest. He always looked at things from his own point of

New York Public Library

OUR JOLLY COOK—CAMPAIGN SKETCHES

New York Public Library

SOLDIERS PLAYING CARDS—CAMPAIGN SKETCHES

Cincinnati Art Museum

CAVALRYMAN (sketch)

Metropolitan Museum of Art

SPRING FARM WORK—GRAFTING

DIAMOND SHOAL

SNAP THE WHIP

view. His best illustrations, therefore, are always those with subjects independently selected by the artist, subjects that represent his natural tastes and interests. And these are the pictures that have the strongest appeal to our interest today, for when left to himself to choose a subject of a picture he invariably selected something simple, something with a timeless human appeal. Many of these pictures suggest the carefree holiday atmosphere of vacation time.

Homer's work in book illustration might be truthfully said to be extremely limited, for actually his illustrations appear in only about two dozen volumes scattered here and there among the work of other artists. There is only one book entirely illustrated by Homer — James Russell Lowell's poem *The Courtin'*, a minor literary effort for which Homer designed a series of illustrations in silhouette, a minor artistic performance, perhaps the perfect complement to the low-keyed charm of the poem. However, although his book illustrations are so very limited in number and his magazine illustrations were obviously a means to an end, they are nonetheless most important and interesting clues to his development as an artist, for there we are able to trace without much guesswork the direct influence upon him of the British illustrators of the 1860's. In fact it is with something of a shock that one comes upon pictures in British magazines that look just exactly like drawings by Homer. The British

Metropolitan Museum of Art

CROQUET PLAYERS

GIRL AND LAUREL

COURSING THE HARE

THE UNRULY CALF

illustrator who exerted the strongest influence on Homer was John Everett Millais — the foremost British artist of that day — but there are traces to be found of the influence of several other important Victorian illustrators and artists — one of the most surprising being Sir Edwin Landseer. Many of his sketches were published in the art magazines of 1870, and some of them, if deprived of their identifying captions, might well be mistaken for Homer's work. Among the other well-known British illustrators of the day whose work must have interested Homer were George Pinwell, Boyd Houghton, Frederick Walker, and the Pre-Raphaelites Dante Gabriel Rossetti and Edward Burne-Jones.

The historian of this group, Gleeson White, says of them: "There can be little doubt that the Pre-Raphaelites gave the first direct impulse to the newer school [of British illustrators in the 1860's] . . . their work, scanty as it is, so far as book illustration is concerned, set going the impulse which in Kelmscott Press . . . and a host of others on both sides of the Atlantic, is 'the movement' of the moment . . . for the Sixties the paramount influence was Millais."

The influence of this new school was immediately felt in America as soon as the new magazines became popular here. Among the leading magazines of this kind were *Once a Week*, *The Cornhill Magazine*, and *Good Words*.

By putting a dozen of Homer's illustrations in chronological order in the period 1859–69 we are enabled to see very clearly the effect of his study of the drawings of those illustrators in England who were creating under the demands of their publishers a whole new style and concept of book and

Mr. and Mrs. Solton Engle

MILKING TIME

magazine illustration. The effect of the new style upon Homer is evident just after the close of the Civil War, and it is especially noticeable in the drawings made in 1868 for the magazine called *Our Young Folks* and for *Appleton's Journal*. These new influences were absorbed, not gradually over a long period, but in a brief space of time, and on his return from Paris late in 1867 the effect of these and other new influences on his work is very marked.

The illustrator and political cartoonist W. A. Rogers in his reminiscences (*A World Worth While*, published in 1922) has some interesting things to say about Winslow Homer the illustrator:

Before the 'seventies there was little real effort on the part of American illustrators to interpret nature. . . . Darley was a man of great talent, but only occasionally did he tear himself away from the old conventional methods. Edwin Forbes came nearer to a true and original style of drawing, but there was no general advance until Abbey and Reinhart set the pace. I verily believe, however, that the first great impulse in the new American art of illustration came from Winslow Homer. When I went to Franklin Square [that is, to work for Harper's in 1877] an occasional drawing on wood still came in for Harper's Weekly from his hand. When one considers how totally different was the style and mode of thought of Homer from Abbey or Reinhart it is hard to believe that they were greatly influenced by him. Nevertheless, he had one quality which he held up before them and which made a deep and lasting impression on the work of both of them. It was in fact the foundation on which their art was built. This was the quality of sincerity. Winslow Homer was perhaps the first American illus-

Mr. and Mrs. Paul Mellon

WAITING FOR DAD

trator to break away from the "slippery" school which balked at the corners in drawing and slid with clever ignorance over every difficulty.

Homer had an artistic sight that was too honest to shirk difficulties. He went straight to nature for his inspiration, and so, in her infinite variety, found new pictures. Abbey and Reinhart were both impressed with the rugged truth of his work, and if one looks at their early illustrations their emancipation from the conventional style of work of that day can readily be seen. It is a very proud fact for an illustrator to reflect upon that one of the greatest masters of painting, recognized the world over, began as a member of his craft.

Metropolitan Museum of Art

WINTER MORNING—SHOVELLING OUT

It will be of interest to any artist who may chance to read this to learn what Homer's drawings were like. I remember one particularly, a drawing on wood. The boxwood color is of a light warm tone and this Homer used as his lightest gray, deepening it with a wash of india ink and painting in one or two highlights with white. There were not more than two or three tones in the picture — just broad flat washes and uncompromising outlines. All that was there was true, but nothing unnecessary or fussy found a place in the drawing. His method was not unlike that of the Japanese artist, Hiroshigi [*sic*]. The subject was a young farmer boy and a girl in a field, a few trees in the background. But that simple picture comes up before me now strong and clear, because of its concentrated and clarified truth.

In reading this estimate of Homer's work it is to be noted that all the things Mr. Rogers admires in it are praised in Ruskinian terms, or praised for Homer's adherence to Pre-Raphaelite principles; for example, "the quality of sincerity"; "he went straight to nature"; the "rugged truth of his work";

"concentrated and clarified truth." And last but not least, his mention of the Japanese print maker Hiroshige is not without significance.

Some of Homer's wood engravings show more plainly than others the influence of his study of the Japanese print maker's style and of the modern British and French art he saw in 1867, but it is perhaps best demonstrated by contrasting his Civil War illustrations with almost any one of those dating after his European trip. The Civil War pictures, though they are full of interest as historical documents, leave much to be desired if they are considered solely as works of art. They lack distinction; the compositions are busy and appear to be unplanned. These prints seldom show any trace or shadow

Metropolitan Museum of Art

WINTER AT SEA—TAKING IN SAIL OFF THE COAST

of the characteristic style we associate in our minds with Winslow Homer. They might in fact have been done by any one of the group of illustrators then working for Harper's. Though some of the faults of these pictures may be laid to the difficulties of making a drawing in the field, and others to the careless translation from drawing to wood block, the main fault lies in the original drawing. The style is simply commonplace, the pictures are like jig-saw puzzles made up of many pieces, each worked out in great detail but related to its neighbors merely by contiguity. The figures are not visualized as interesting groups composed with care, each one is merely an isolated detail in a mass of other details. The planes of the picture are crudely cut, like the successive flats of a scene painter in the theater — the foreground figures are large and dark, the middle distance is lighter and smaller, and the distance fades off into a welter of little mules or tents or stereotyped tree shapes. This is, in a word, not art but rather poor pictorial journalism. It is an unselective reporting of a mass of facts,

Canajoharie Library and Art Gallery

HOMEWORK

NEW ENGLAND COUNTRY SCHOOL

BREAKWATER, TYNEMOUTH

there is no doubt that all the things seen in the picture are true and all were visible, but they were seen by a journeyman who had not learned how to transform pictorial facts into meaningful artistic truths.

Compare any of these prints with the work he was doing after his return from Paris. Take the *Skating* print of 1868 and contrast it with *A Bivouac Fire on the Potomac,* published in 1861, or *Halt of a Wagon Train,* published in 1864, and the change in feeling is plainly evident. What has happened? Homer has learned to design a picture, his experiences abroad have transformed him from an ordinary illustrator into an artist. He has been changed from a callow apprentice, a run-of-the-mill newspaper illustrator into a designer, a print maker, a master workman who knows what he wants to do and how to do it.

What a pity it is that no enterprising publisher had the wit to ask Homer to illustrate *Huckleberry Finn* or *Tom Sawyer* — think what a monument that would have been. Or how felicitously he could have illustrated some of the Boston novels of William Dean Howells.

Considering the complete lists of his illustrations, the subjects seem to fall into three general categories, and by far the largest one is that which might be called vacation-time activities — husking bees, picnics, bathing, fishing, sailing, camping out, hunting, skating, berrying, the straw ride, the sleigh ride, the apple bee. The second-largest group of subjects would be the Civil War scenes; all the rest fall into a miscellany of rather tame Boston and New York street scenes, some trifling scenes from a tiresome novel, the odds and ends of city life down to the dregs of a Chinese opium den in New York. It is easy to see where Homer's real interests lie, and why after his apprenticeship he always refused to tie himself down to a regular job, preferring always the uncertainty of independence because of its reward of absolute freedom.

Indeed the greater part of his life seems to have been a vacation, and his work as an artist — in watercolor at any rate — was a congenial form of vacation pastime.

This vacation note is perhaps one of the main keys to Homer's character and to the enduring popularity of his work. He escaped from the city on every possible occasion, and as soon as he was financially able to do so he established himself permanently in residence at a summer resort. And from this permanent vacation on the coast of Maine, where he lived for the last twenty-seven years of his life, he set out on seasonal vacations to the Adirondacks in summer, or in winter to the Bahamas or Florida.

Homer's vacation subjects not only reflect his own inclinations and pleasures in the open air of the sea and countryside; they also reflect a growing trend in American life of the time. In the post-Civil War period more and more Americans found the time in summer for a country vacation, a ramble in the White Mountains, or a stay at the seashore.

Homer's work as an illustrator, carried on for about seventeen years, inevitably had the most profound effect upon his greater works — his paintings. The most obvious effect, of course, was in his choice of subject. He had little interest in pure landscape; with few exceptions his pictures were concerned with people until late in his career, when he became engrossed with his study of the sea. His pictures, like most good illustrations — and like most good Victorian paintings — are primarily concerned with ideas rather than purely aesthetic problems.

CANOE IN RAPIDS

SHOOTING THE RAPIDS, SAGUENAY RIVER

AFTER THE HURRICANE, BAHAMAS

UNDER THE COCO PALM

THE SIGNAL OF DISTRESS (sketch)

EIGHT BELLS (etching)

CHAPTER SEVEN

HOMER AND THE "ETCHING CRAZE," 1866-96

"Etching was originally a diversion of the studio . . . Among artists it possessed a high value. To the public at large it had practically none . . . It remained for accident to give it popularity . . . Accident in this country . . . assumed the guise of Dr. Seymour Haden. The visit of this able amateur, and the attention given him by the press, made the art he pleaded for a fashion. From fashion to folly is a facile step."
ALFRED TRUMBLE — *Etching in America,* 1887

TODAY IT IS NOT generally remembered that in the thirty years from 1866 to 1896, there arose, flourished, and declined what has been called "the etching craze." The curious history of this phenomena has not recently been explored by students of American art because in recent years there has been a notable lack of interest in the art of etching and practically no interest at all in the American etchings produced in such quantities in this thirty-year period. These etchings, with very few exceptions, have not yet reclaimed the attention of critics or collectors or historians of American art. However, since Homer was, for a brief period, affected by the general mania for etching, it may be interesting to trace to its sources in Europe the beginnings of this forgotten episode in American art and by outlining its course in America to show Homer's relation to the movement in general.

The interest in the so-called "painter etchings" that arose in France and in England after 1860 can be attributed to the action of a few potent causes and the reaction of a few influential men who were in a position to make their ideas effective among artists. The principal cause of the renewed interest in etching was actually the encroachment of the camera and the photomechanical processes for reproducing pictures into what had formerly been the exclusive domain of the artist. Another potent influence in arousing interest in etching came from the ideas about the art expressed by two of the leading art critics of the time; Charles Baudelaire and Théophile Gautier. Important as these men and factors were, there was M. Cadart, who perhaps did more to organize and sustain the movement than any other single person in Paris. He was a publisher of prints, an amateur etcher, who exhibited, sold, and talked etching with boundless enthusiasm.

In 1863 Cadart, prompted by a suggestion of the etcher Alphonse Legros, founded the Société des Aquafortistes. This was started partly to act as a gathering place and center for artists who wished to protest against the arbitrary judgments of the Salon jury — and partly to provide Cadart with an excuse to issue a series of modern etchings as the publications of the Société. In a note in the first volume of this publication the critic Gautier stated the case for the Aquafortistes. He says:

At this time when photography charms the mob by the mechanical fidelity of its reproductions, it is necessary to encourage an artistic trend in favor of free caprice and picturesque fantasy. The need to react against the positivism of the mirror-like camera has forced more than one painter to take to the etcher's needle; the unification of these men of talent, annoyed at seeing the walls [of the Salon] tapestried with monotone images from which the soul is absent, now form the Société des Aqua-fortistes . . . the etchings reproduce exactly each trace drawn by the artist . . . in them one has the very idea of the master, pulsing with life and spontaneity . . . The Société has no other code than individu-alism. Each must invent and engrave . . . one is free to show all the originality one has . . . The Société des Aquafortistes was founded precisely to combat photography, lithography, aqua-tint, and engrav-ings . . . to combat regular, automatic work, without inspiration which denatures the very idea of the artist . . .

Baudelaire, like Gautier, also thought highly of the etching because it gave "the most clean-cut possible translation of the character of the artist." Baudelaire was attracted by those who were reviving the art of etching, because they gave clear proof in their work of that personal force and distinction that he valued above all else and that he was always on the alert to discover in the productions of the new and the unknown.

This revival of interest in etchings among artists and critics, collectors, publishers, and dealers and among their literary friends in Paris spurred a revival of interest in etching among English artists, and the influence of this French and English enthusiasm for the art was quickly transferred to the artists of the United States. The transfer was effected principally through the influence of only a

Metropolitan Museum of Art

SAVED

PERILS OF THE SEA (etching)

few men. American artists, who were then becoming more sensitive to new movements in the European art world, were initiated into the fine points of the art of etching by none other than M. Cadart himself, who came to New York in 1866 to exhibit modern French etchings, to sell etcher's supplies and subscriptions to the publications of the Société des Aquafortistes. His enthusiasm for etching resulted in the foundation of a New York branch of the société, but on his departure for Paris this little organization fell apart. Cadart's influence, however powerful it may have been on a few American artists at that time, was principally of value as an opening wedge — a beginning — an initiation for both the public and the artists to the beauty of etching.

Another Frenchman who had a certain influence among American etchers was Maxime Lalanne, whose treatise on etching was translated into English and published in Boston in 1880. Another man influential in introducing the etching craze in America was Whistler, one of the first Americans to take up the new art in Paris in the late 1850's. The notice his etchings received in London and Paris reverberated with effect at home. Whistler's British brother-in-law, Seymour Haden, the famous surgeon and amateur etcher, was another influential figure.

The large display of foreign and American etchings at the Centennial Exposition in Philadelphia in 1876 further stimulated the general interest in the art and resulted in the following year in the foundation of the New York Etching Club. Shortly thereafter similar clubs were organized in Philadelphia, Boston, Chicago, and Cincinnati.

WATCHING THE BREAKERS

THE WRECK OF THE *IRON CROWN*

WRECKED SCHOONER

THE WRECK

Perhaps the most significant encouragement to the art of etching in America was provided in 1881, when the Boston Museum of Fine Arts held its exhibition of the work of American etchers — an exhibition in which over four hundred American etchings were displayed with a choice selection of European work. In that same year many American etchers received what they considered the accolade when they were invited to show their work in London at the first exhibition of the Society of Painter-Etchers, organized by Seymour Haden.

In the winter of 1882–83, Haden came to the United States to deliver a series of lectures on etching in New York, Philadelphia, Boston, Detroit, and Chicago. The American press gave his tour, his lectures, and his social activities (which might include several more or less acrimonious arguments about etching) the very fullest coverage, and when Haden returned to England everyone in America who could read a newspaper was aware of the art of etching and knew that a famous British swell who advocated the art had been upon our shores. The etching craze then burst into full flower. Every painter was experimenting with etching, a whole tribe of collectors of etchings appeared, and with them came a group of dealers in prints to supply the demand.

Though Haden's visit made etchings fashionable (and the collection of etchings became almost an obligation for every well-bred gentleman then) and though he brought the art to the attention of a wide audience of potential buyers and collectors of etchings, his influence among American artists and makers of etchings was never so important as that of Philip Gilbert Hamerton. Haden's influence on collectors ultimately resulted, not in the building up of collections of etchings by American artists, but in the collection of etchings by Haden, Whistler, and the work of the popular French etchers of the time. Thus today some of our public print collections have almost every print in every state made by some French artists, and complete sets of Haden's and Whistler's prints, but it is rare to find a complete set of etchings by Winslow Homer in any print collection.

Metropolitan Museum of Art

SAVED

Metropolitan Museum of Art

MENDING THE NETS (etching)

Though Baudelaire, Gautier, Cadart, Lalanne, Haden, and Whistler all had their influence on American etchers of the time, none of these men can lay claim to the direct and powerful kind of influence exercised by the British critic and author Philip Gilbert Hamerton (1834–94), who wrote the standard handbooks on the history and techniques of etching. In the last decades of the nineteenth century his influence among practicing artists was much greater than that of Ruskin, and in America no artist or writer on art had more influence in the post-Civil War period than he had.

Although he is now almost completely forgotten (except perhaps in the small select circle of those who still collect etchings), he was in the last thirty or forty years of the nineteenth century the most widely read and most respected writer on art. His influence through his numerous handbooks on the various phases and techniques of the art of his time is not to be underestimated. From 1870 to the time of his death he was editor and one of the principal contributors to *The Portfolio*, one of the leading art periodicals of the day. This magazine — inspired by the success of Cadart's publication in Paris — with its adventurous experiments in utilizing various new methods of illustration, and most particularly for its use of original etchings especially commissioned as illustrations, immediately took precedence over older art periodicals that were illustrated solely with engravings on wood or on steel. *The Portfolio* and the ideas of its editor had a profound effect on its readers, both professional artists and connoisseurs. Hamerton's books and his magazine were particularly significant elements in starting or supporting certain trends in the sudden growth of general interest in art that took place in the United States after the close of the Civil War. It was due to Hamerton that there was a whole school of etchers and a group of collectors of etchings in America. One writer of the time says:

> I think it hardly possible to over-estimate the effect of Mr. Hamerton's writings. In January 1866, he published an article upon etching in the Fine Arts Quarterly Review and in 1868 appeared the first edition of his *Etchers and Etching*. I deem it no exaggeration to say that the modern revival of etching has been due very largely to this book.

Though Hamerton is perhaps tediously pedantic in explaining and describing the finest points of the technical processes for making an etching, and his book is full of the kind of sound practical advice that answers in the most detailed manner all the questions a student etcher might ask, there can be little doubt that his book was a source of inspiration for hundreds of American artists. The author's stolid seriousness gave his writing the humorless, admonitory tone of lessons to be memorized by recalcitrant students. However, serious as his books on art were, they were always well written. His first book on painting was one of the most successful art books of the period, titled *A Painter's Camp*, first published in 1862, which gave accounts of his sketching trips in Scotland, England, and in France. This book is full of interesting observations and can still be read today with pleasure, for he can tell an interesting story and his Ruskinian study of nature in the Scottish highlands gives one a fair sample of the kinds of things young artists were thinking about in the late 1850's. He details his adventures in the mountains and high moorlands of Scotland where he painted landscapes and studied effects of light. He describes the equipment he took along on this sketching trip, some of it rather elaborate — for instance, his portable painting hut with its plate-glass window, which allowed him to work in the most inclement weather. (This was an idea that Homer later adopted for his own use while painting on the Maine coast in winter.)

Another feature of Hamerton's book was his careful effort to explain to unbelieving Scottish crofters, shepherds, and innkeepers just what he was doing. His idea of camping out seemed to them utterly mad, and most of them could not understand what a painting was. His friends at home were only little less astonished — in the first place camping out was unheard of in England unless one was forced to do so by accident or on some military expedition in the colonies. The general Philistine attitude toward art and artists is well displayed here, and Hamerton's patient explanations of what he hoped to accomplish by this novel means of study must have been enlightening experience for hundreds of his readers on both sides of the Atlantic.

Although all of Hamerton's books were popular in the United States — perhaps even more popular than they were in England — the books that were most generally read by American artists and art lovers were *A Painter's Camp* already described and his remarkable handbook *Etching and Etchers*, first published in 1868. This book immediately became the standard reference book on the subject and it went through many editions. Even today it still is a useful book, though some of his critical estimates are not in accord with modern tastes (he was too matter of fact to understand the fantastic etchings of Goya). But in spite of such lapses there is no phase of the history or the technique of etching that is not fully treated in this book. It even provides the collector of etchings with a list of important works he should seek for his collection and gives detailed instructions for storing the collection in specially built cabinets.

Among his other books were *The Handbook of Etching*, 1871; *The Graphic Arts*, 1882; *The Life of J. M. W. Turner*, 1879; *Thoughts about Art*, 1871; *Imagination in Landscape Painting*, 1887;

STOWING SAILS, BAHAMAS

THE PUMPKIN PATCH—HARVEST SCENE

BOY FISHING

NORTHWOODS (Prang chromolithograph)

OLD FRIENDS

Drawing and Engraving, 1892; *The Unknown River, an Etcher's Voyage of Discovery,* 1870; *The Present State of the Fine Arts in France,* 1892; *Examples of Modern Etchings,* 1876.

By 1880, Hamerton's books and his magazine had made such a name for him that each new book as it came out was greeted with enthusiasm. In the later 1880's complete sets of Hamerton's works in fourteen volumes bound in calf were being sold in Boston and New York bookshops for fifty-six dollars the set. In Hamerton's autobiography the large sale of his books in America is mentioned, with especial gratitude for the royalties received from his Boston publisher, Roberts Brothers.

One cannot say in so many words that the writings of Hamerton on etching, on camping, and on landscape painting were read by Homer and that they influenced him. However, Hamerton's writings had such a wide audience in America, and there was at the time so little else published in America about contemporary art, it would be a mistake to think that Hamerton's ideas and enthusiasms were not known to Homer even as they were probably known to every other American artist of the time. The good word about his books spread from one studio to another as each delighted reader expressed his pleasure in Hamerton's informative and entertaining way of writing about his adventures. Of course camping out was not the novelty for Americans that it must have been for proper Victorian Englishmen. However, in the case of Hamerton's books on etching, they furnished the inspiration and the necessary information that made it possible for Homer and his fellow artists to take up the pursuit. In fact Homer himself says that he learned about etching from books and by studying the works of

Metropolitan Museum of Art

EASTERN SHORE (Prang chromolithograph)

BURNT MOUNTAIN

RANGER IN THE ADIRONDACKS

the other etchers who had their prints proved on Ritchie's etching press or in Klackner's shop.

Among the first American artists to become seriously interested in etching were two of Homer's oldest friends — Joseph Baker and J. Foxcroft Cole. It is most probable that Homer was introduced to the art by Cole when Homer was in Paris, though he is not known to have produced any finished plates until sometime in the 1880's.

Actually Homer took up the new art rather late and he appears to have thought of etching solely as a means of making salable reproductions of his paintings. There is no evidence that he practiced the art of etching as a free and direct mode of making pictures independent of his previous studies in oil or watercolor.

All of Homer's etchings were made in the years from about 1883 to about 1889. His complete output in this medium is generally considered to consist of eight etchings. Their titles will recall Homer's paintings of the same subjects:

> *Eight Bells*
> *Saved (The Life Line)*
> *Saved (The Life Line)* (etched on a larger plate than the first issue)
> *Mending the Nets*
> *Perils of the Sea*
> *Undertow*
> *A Voice from the Cliffs*
> *Fly Fishing, Saranac*

Brooklyn Museum

BOATMAN

PALM TREE, NASSAU

TAKING ON WET PROVISIONS

THE TURTLE POUND

After 1888 all these plates were printed by Christian Klackner of New York and published and sold by him. Most of them were issued in two different formats — on parchment paper at thirty dollars each, and on Japan paper at twenty dollars each.

The classic anecdote about Homer's etchings is told by J. Eastman Chase in his "Recollections of Winslow Homer." He writes:

> His view of the attitude of the public toward his work was sometimes rather whimsical . . . as an illustration of this whimsical view of what he believed to be the vagaries of the public taste, let me give this letter dated Scarboro, Maine, May 14, 1888:
>
>> "I have an idea for next winter, if what I am now engaged on is a success and Mr. K. is agreeable. That is to exhibit an oil painting . . . with an etching from it, with a pretty girl at the desk to sell."

As far as we know Homer never made any etchings that were independent of his paintings. His etchings were in effect reproductions. Yet Homer did exhibit at the New York Etching Club in 1889 a print rather mysteriously titled *Improve the Shining Hour* — a title that does not fit well with the subject of any of his known etchings. Perhaps this plate was an experiment that was not successful in its final state and was later destroyed, though it could conceivably be an alternative title for *Mending the Nets*.

Homer's etchings seem to have had only a very brief moment of popularity and they have since

Metropolitan Museum of Art

FLY FISHING, SARANAC

HIGH TIDE: THE BATHERS

the middle 1890's suffered the same ignominious fate that has been meted out to all the other big etchings of that day. Today no one seems to care much what has happened to all these grand treasures, so vast in size with their creamy margins punctuated with apt remarques or vignettes. Where all those signed artist's proofs on elegant sheets of handmade paper? They seem to have all passed into a sort of limbo for unloved art objects, and the change in taste seems to have swept away the etched work of Homer as well as of all the rest.

To some tastes his etchings are much less impressive than his paintings, yet Homer himself always considered them among his best work. Perhaps he felt this way about them because he put so much time and effort into making the plates — a proper no-nonsense New England attitude. But to others it seems that the mechanical aspects of reproducing a painting by etching — the cold plate, the sharp gravers and needles, the vials of acid, and the weighty press — interposed too many unsympathetic elements between the artist and his work. In any case, when the etchings didn't sell, Homer quite properly lost interest in making them. This accounts for his small output in this medium.

It is a curious fact that the photograph and photomechanical processes of reproducing printed pictures, which spurred the revival of interest in etchings among the artists of the middle nineteenth century, were also responsible in the last decade of the century for bringing the revival of etching to a close. By the end of the century color printing processes had made it possible to make printed copies of paintings in full color, making the reproduction of paintings by means of etching absolutely obsolete. And the photogravure reproduction of etchings and paintings made the production of pictures of this kind so cheap and so plentiful the art of etching lost its appeal to most artists because they could no longer derive any income from it. There were of course certain dedicated artists who continued their work as etchers because they liked the medium, but in general the photogravure and the chromolithographic printing processes brought "the etching craze" to a sudden halt.

Minneapolis Institute of Arts

CONCH DIVERS

HUDSON RIVER, LOGGING

THE ARTIST'S STUDIO IN AN AFTERNOON FOG

IN THE MOUNTAINS

AFTER THE HUNT

THE HERRING NET

CHAPTER EIGHT

HOMER'S MASTERPIECES

*"Nothing astonishes men so much as common sense and plain dealing.
All great actions have been simple, and all great pictures are."*

EMERSON, *Art*

IN ORDER to get some idea of the tremendous impact made by Homer's paintings when they were first exhibited, one should examine the illustrations in the exhibition catalogues of the time, or consider some of the paintings chosen to illustrate the books on American painting that were published in the 1890's and just after the turn of the century. It is only then that one can begin to realize how stark and imposing, how strong and unconventional, how individual and impressive Homer's pictures must have appeared. To a generation of art lovers and critics whose tastes had been nurtured on the sweet confections imported from Düsseldorf or Paris, or on the careful *nature morte* landscapes of minor Hudson River painters and the peppermint patties turned out by Will Low and his bohemian friends in the Society of American Artists, Homer's pictures must have seemed like the work of a rude barbarian. To the tender-minded Homer's works appeared gross, brutal, austere, unfinished, if not downright ugly — just the way Manet appeared to his critics in the 1860's. Homer's pictures by contrast now allow us to realize to the full the bland banality, the true vulgarity of the work of many of his contemporaries. Yet many of these men were at the time considered to be among the leading American artists, the masters, the geniuses of the day, the ornaments of their profession.

During his lifetime Homer was subjected to a certain amount of critical balderdash from the reviewers of exhibitions and the writers of essays and books on American art. These naturally never had the slightest effect upon the artist, and he serenely pursued his self-set course oblivious to the cries of pain or outrage that his pictures drew from those who demanded nothing from painters but multiplied saccharinities. Though Homer ignored the criticisms of professional reviewers and art critics, he listened with attention to the terse comments about his marine pictures from Grand Banks fishermen or from the local lobstermen around Prouts Neck — they knew what they were talking about and their perception of his paintings was not obscured by any aesthetic fogs. To Homer a painting was a means of communicating an idea and for him a painting was a failure when the viewer did not understand the meaning of his picture. He was concerned only secondarily with the aesthetic means by which this communication was accomplished — these were solely the concern of the artist and should properly be hidden.

An old-fashioned critic who concealed himself under a pen name, "Outremer," published a long tirade on the American art exhibition at the Universal Exposition in Paris in 1878 (in *The Aldine,* Vol. IX). Practically everything about the show outraged him. He complains that the jury of selection consisted of only one man. He didn't like the paintings by Vedder — "bad in drawing, in composition and in color"; work by his favorite artist Frederick E. Church was "skyed"; "two of the worst painted landscapes in the exhibition are signed G. Inness"; "F. A. Bridgeman's 'Funeral on the Nile in the Days of the Pharaohs' is without exception the best picture in the collection." Homer's contribution to the show consisted of the following paintings: *On the Bright Side, The Visit from the Old Mistress, Sunday Morning in Virginia, New England Country School,* and *Snap the Whip.* Of these paintings Outremer writes:

> Another of those "buds of promise" occupying "the line" . . . is Winslow Homer. What excuse can the painter offer for sending, and our judge and jury for accepting, under the head of Fine Arts, such nondescripts as those which bear Mr. Homer's name?

This rather bitter comment shows how alarming, how disturbing a fresh point of view, an individual manner of painting, an unaccustomed choice of subject can be to conventional-minded critics and art lovers. This particular critic seems to be exceptionally annoyed with this exhibition of American painting because so much valuable space "on the line" was given to the work of the men of a younger generation whose greatest faults were that they were new talents and their pictures were well displayed instead of being "skyed" or hung in dark corridors, where the works of new young painters, at least in the estimation of Outremer, should be hung. But gradually changes took place in the general tone of the critical comments made about the new paintings, and though Homer's pictures were frequently criticized on one ground or another, most critics in future cannot refrain from ending their remarks about him with something complimentary.

Mrs. Thomas Hitchcock

EVENING ON THE BEACH

PALM TREES, FLORIDA

LOST ON THE GRAND BANKS

In the 1880's the attitude of some American art critics toward Homer began to change, and in them we find reflected the ideas Ruskin and some of the leading French critics of the 1880's — the ideas that had formed the philosophical basis upon which the artists of the modern movement of the 1860's had founded their work. For instance in the account of the annual exhibition at the National Academy of Design in 1886 the critic of the *Art Review* writes:

> Winslow Homer shows in his *Lost on the Grand Banks* a rude vigor and grim force that is almost a tonic in the midst of the namby-pambyism of many of the other pictures. The utter simplicity of the composition, the fidelity to local coloring (and Mr. Homer's peculiar gamut of color never seemed more appropriate), and the spirited rendering of the wave-tossed boat and its anxious occupants — these are elements characteristic of Mr. Homer's work, but always welcome because Mr. Homer always has something to say.

Further evidence of the penetration of new European ideas into the atmosphere of the New York art world is revealed in the account of on the National Academy show of 1887. This appears with special clarity in the critical comment on Homer's contribution to the exhibition, and it also shows the indelible impression his work left in the minds of those who studied his pictures. The critic writes:

> The emptiness of these pictures is no more characteristic of the Academy exhibition than of others, but they seem more bloodless than ever here after the superb virility of Mr. Winslow Homer's *Undertow.* Two women . . . are being rescued by two stalwart coast-guardsmen. . . . One . . . is towing them by ropes . . . the second rescuer stoops to lift the heavy folds of a dress which retards progress. The first is half nude, his muscles as distinct and tense after the strain as those of an oarsmen "well

SEARCHLIGHT, HARBOR ENTRANCE, SANTIAGO DE CUBA

trained down" at the end of a hard-pulled race. His figure is modeled as cleanly and solidly as sculpture in the round, and his companion with clothing torn off and cut in strips by the struggle with the waves is another finely plastic figure . . . Just beyond these four figures a wave rises in an emerald arch . . . One can find fault with drawing, texture and color in Mr. Homer's picture, and yet come away from the exhibition and think of nothing else. For there is a quality here above and beyond technique, a vigorous individuality, a man and a strong thought behind the picture.

Homer is frequently criticized for faulty drawing, for coarse textures, and for peculiar color, as he is here, but despite these Pre-Raphaelite faults, whether real or imaginary, the critic usually admits, as it happens in this case, that Homer's contribution to the exhibition is really the only memorable one. In effect they are saying that Homer is that "powerful individual" Zola called for in 1867 "who knows how to create, along-side God's world, a personal world which my eyes will never be able to forget and which they will recognize anywhere."

Perhaps the most noted of all his critics was the youthful Henry James, who, in a now famous passage in a review of the art season of 1875 (published in the July issue of *The Galaxy*,) makes the following remarks:

Few of the painters represented at the Academy did much in the way of winning from us an expenditure of fancy and ingenuity. The most striking pictures in the exhibition were perhaps those of Mr. Homer; and this artist certainly can rarely have had occasion to complain of being judged with too much subtlety. Before Mr. Homer's little barefoot urchins and little girls in calico sun-bonnets,

straddling beneath a cloudless sky upon the national rail fence, the whole effort of the critic is instinc-
tively to contract himself, to double himself up, as it were, so that he can creep into the problem and
examine it humbly and patiently, if a trifle wonderingly. Mr. Homer's pictures, in other words, imply
no explanatory sonnets; the artist turns his back squarely and frankly upon literature. In this he may
be said to be typical of the general body of his fellow artists. . . . What we say here of the Academy
we may extend to the annual Water-Color Exhibition, which almost immediately preceded it. The
Water-Color Exhibition was, relatively speaking, a brighter show than that made by the Academicians;
but the best pictures there (contributed by native artists at least) were the simplest — those which
attempted least. There too Mr. Homer was in force; and in his little raw aquarelles, as well as in
several specimens of the infinitely finer and more intellectual, but still narrow and single-toned work
of Miss Fidelia Bridges, we found perhaps, among the American performances, our best entertain-
ment. The most interesting things, however, were not American. These consisted of some four elabo-
rately finished pictures by Mrs. Spartali Stillman, who works in England, under the shadow of Messrs.
Burne Jones and Rossetti. . . .
Of Mr. Homer's three pictures we have spoken, but there would be a good deal more to say about
them; not, we mean, because they are particularly important in themselves, but because they are
peculiarly typical. A frank, absolute, sincere expression of any tendency is always interesting, even

Cooper Union Museum

THE HERRING NET (study)

Museum of Fine Arts, Boston

A HAUL OF HERRING

when the tendency is not elevated or the individual not distinguished. Mr. Homer goes in, as the phrase is, for perfect realism, and cares not a jot for such fantastic hair-splitting as the distinction between beauty and ugliness. He is a genuine painter; that is, to see, and to reproduce what he sees, is his only care; to think, to imagine, to select, to refine, to compose, to drop into any of the intellectual tricks with which other people sometimes try to eke out the dull pictorial vision — all this Mr. Homer triumphantly avoids. He not only has no imagination, but he contrives to elevate this rather blighting negative into a blooming and honorable positive. He is almost barbarously simple, and to our eye, he is horribly ugly; but there is nevertheless something one likes about him. What is it? For ourselves, it is not his subjects. We frankly confess that we detest his subjects — his barren plank fences, his glaring, bald blue skies, his big, dreary, vacant lots of meadows, his freckled straight-haired Yankee urchins, his flat-breasted maidens, suggestive of a dish of rural doughnuts and pie, his calico sun-bonnets, his flannel shirts, his cow-hide boots. He has chosen the least pictorial features of the least pictorial range of scenery and civilization; he has resolutely treated them as if they were pictorial, as if they were every inch as good as Capri or Tangiers; and, to reward his audacity, he has incontestably succeeded. It makes one feel the value of consistency; it is a proof that if you will only be doggedly literal, though you may often be unpleasing, you will at least have a stamp of your own. Mr. Homer has the great merit, moreover, that he naturally sees everything at one with its envelope of light and air. He sees not in lines, but in masses, in gross, broad masses. Things come already modelled to his eye. If his masses were only sometimes a trifle more broken, and his brush a good deal richer — if it had a good many more secrets and mysteries and coquetries, he would be, with his vigorous way of looking and seeing, even if fancy in the matter remained the same dead blank, an almost distinguished painter. In its suggestion of this blankness of fancy the picture

THE LIFE LINE

of the young farmer flirting with the pie-nurtured maiden in the wheat field is really an intellectual curiosity. The want of grace, of intellectual detail, of reflected light, could hardly go further; but the picture was its author's best contribution, and a very honest, and vivid, and manly piece of work. Our only complaint with it is that it is damnably ugly! We spoke just now of Mr. La Farge, and it occurs to us that the best definition of Mr. Homer to the initiated would be, that he is an elaborate contradiction of Mr. La Farge. In the Palace of Art there are many mansions!

What Mr. James seems to want are all the fashionable things that tastes trained on European paintings seemed to think were virtues. He is unfortunately cornered by Homer's inescapable power and individuality, which allow the artist to triumph over all difficulties and all lacks, his lack of urbane polish, his lack of "rich brushwork," of "secrets," of "mysteries and coquetries," yet, though Homer lacked all these fashionable attributes, James must in the end grudgingly admit him to be an "almost distinguished painter" even in 1875, before his greatest paintings had been put on canvas. What appears to James to be "damnably ugly" in Homer's paintings is now one of their principal charms. It seems to us quite capricious on the part of the critic to suggest that Homer lacks imagination; the difficulty really lies in the lack of imagination of the critic who looks for superficial artistic effects and, missing them, complains that more serious and more subtle qualities are also missing. James is actually accusing Homer of not being a fashionable French painter.

His remarks that the painting of a "young farmer flirting with the pie-nurtured maiden in the wheat field" is "an intellectual curiosity" reveal the curiously provincial attitude of the critic, and

THE FOG WARNING

one feels that it was also the attitude of the many Americans who thought Homer crude and "damnably ugly." These were the very people who went mad over the sententious peasants of Millet. Perhaps a sophisticate like Henry James could patronize, in his imagination, the foreign peasants, so lowly, so devout, and so like their own oxen, plodding and mild. But not even Mr. James could patronize an American farmer, damnably ugly though he might be, nor could he sentimentalize over the flat-breasted sunbonneted American farm girl who might after all marry a millionaire barbed-wire salesman and end her days in style at Newport. Something that could never happen to Millet's bovine clods.

Perhaps we have all become so accustomed to this rural-doughnut-and-apple-pie gambit, in considering Homer's art, we have been overlooking the unique combination of American, European, and Asiatic elements in his pictures. We have forgotten the importance of the oriental spices that bring out in these typically American comestibles their distinctive native flavor.

It is an interesting commentary on the evolutions and reverses in American taste during the past hundred years to see that once again Homer's early pictures — the simple rustic scenes — now command more attention than those grandiloquent marine compositions that were at one time considered to be his most important contribution to American art. His pictures seem now to be valued principally for the very things Henry James deplores. One does not look at a picture like *Breezing Up* (painted in 1876) to savor its rich brushwork or its poetic mystery; it is seen now as a picture that sparkles with the joy of sailing — a picture that makes a definitive statement about boys and boats and breezes; to modern eyes its subtle artistic qualities, its buoyant and lively composition, reward the eye in a way that the soft French clichés of the 1870's cannot now match.

Only shortly after Mr. James complains of Homer's choice of the "damnably ugly" homely

American subject matter and his lack of the smooth, sweet skills that marked the works of so many European painters, as well as those of so many of the European-trained Americans, another critic remarks:

> If our [American] artists have shown a stunted development on the side of imaginativeness and originality, it is because they have willfully chosen to sell their birthright for foreign importations. They have been and they are still groping, wandering, and seeking through a hundred different avenues the road to producing something original *in a foreign tongue*. In other words they are content with painting and repainting French subjects, according to French methods, for an American public. And yet here is our own landscape, in all its glory and freshness, its meaning as yet scarcely guessed by the few Wyants and Innesses and Bolton Jonses who have had the courage and the loyalty to study its character and to embody its sentiment and its fairness through the medium of large ideas. The same is true of our life and our people. The field is almost untouched. America, in relation to its art, is still the Sphinx awaiting the idealist who shall read aloud her secrets.

How this writer lost an opportunity to list Winslow Homer among the artists who were beginning to guess at the meaning of the glorious fresh American landscapes one does not know, for Homer was much more American — or perhaps one should say, much less Europeanized — as a painter, than Alexander Wyant, George Inness, or H. Bolton Jones — all of them being at that time fairly strongly influenced by the French painters of the Barbizon school.

Homer seems to have always been unusually lucky in the sale of his paintings from the very beginning of his career. Though he was not immediately rewarded with high prices, his luck was marked by the influential character of the men who bought his pictures. This in itself gave Homer's work a special note of distinction in some circles. For instance, his first really important picture *Prisoners from the Front*, first exhibited in New York in 1866, was bought from the exhibition by John Taylor Johnston, an important businessman whose great interest in art resulted in his becoming a founder and first president of the Metropolitan Museum of Art in 1870. The sale of this picture not only financed Homer's trip to Paris, but since his work had gained such hearty approval from such a prominent connoisseur and collector, it gave the young artist a new standing in the community and made him a man to be watched.

The Civil War picture *Prisoners from the Front* is said to have caused a sensation when it was exhibited at the National Academy in 1866. Today it appears to be a most interesting picture, but certainly it cannot be considered very sensational. Aside from feelings that might arise from its political or military aspects one would not say that the painting was especially dramatic and it certainly is not shocking. Its color is sober, its composition is rather static, the picture seems to be a sedate illustration competently done. Perhaps one important clue to its initial success at the academy can be disclosed by a mere glance at the titles of the other paintings in the show, for they alone betray their commonplace nature as works of sentiment and prettiness. By making this contrast it is easy to see how Homer's picture — a painting that made a bold, simple statement — when placed in a gallery full of insipid sunsets and "fancy pieces," would dominate the whole exhibition. The artist must have appeared as an eagle among sparrows, a new, unique talent, strong and truthful, masculine and virtuous. The painting is of course essentially Pre-Raphaelite in character — it is a simple, direct statement of honest fact about modern life.

Homer's paintings appealed to men and most of them were bought by prosperous and substantial merchants, lawyers, and businessmen who admired in art the simple direct and unsentimental pictures of pleasing and interesting subjects that Homer knew so well how to produce. His pictures were for

A WALL, NASSAU

FLOWER GARDEN AND BUNGALOW, BERMUDA

THE TWO GUIDES (Detail)

the most part of subjects that would appeal to growing numbers of men who found time to desert Wall Street or State Street for summer vacations and for fishing and hunting trips. Perhaps the most powerful of all of these was the retired banker Thomas B. Clarke, who through his many connections in the business world and in the special world of the New York club man of 1890 did more to spread the good word about Homer among men of this class than any other person.

Among the prominent men who bought Homer's paintings in the 1890's and just after the turn of the century were the New Yorkers Charles W. Gould, a man of great wealth; Edward D. Adams, an industrialist, promoter, and organizer of international business schemes; Samuel Untermyer, and Joseph Choate, both powerful lawyers; and Dr. Lewis Stimson, the surgeon. In Philadelphia the art-collecting lawyer John G. Johnson and the financier Edward T. Stotesbury both owned paintings by Homer. In Boston, Edward Hooper, treasurer of Harvard College and a trustee of the Boston Museum of Fine Arts, collected Homers; and there were of course many others who might be mentioned, such as Charles L. Freer, the Detroit capitalist and collector of oriental art and Whistlers.

Homer's work appeared to be without any of those deceptive aesthetic frills and flourishes that characterized the work of so many fashionable European painters and their American imitators. It did not inspire the kind of self-conscious art jargon of the "higher criticism" or the kind of art chatter that often passed for criticism in artistic circles; the kind of talk that so many American men found baffling, nebulous, and vaguely effeminate. His pictures were never calculated to shock or alarm by intriguing hints of Parisian sensuality or by any taint of radical bohemian ideas.

Perhaps one of the strongest attractions Homer's pictures had for those who collected his paintings was their appeal to that powerful hankering of many American men for the deep woods. This

Clark Art Institute

THE TWO GUIDES

was in part an undyingly boyish desire to play at being carefree wild Indians, but it was also an effort — a fairly successful effort — to escape, like Huck Finn, from the dominance of women and their everlasting, sanctimonious preachers who played such a great part in American cultural and domestic life in the nineteenth century. The robust delights of fishing for trout in the Canadian wilderness, the solitude of the deserted summer resort, the unfashionable excursions to Florida and the Bahamas under sail in small boats held little charm for most women of the later nineteenth century. It was a man's world that Homer painted, the adventurous world of the sportsman fraught with real excitement even if it was an excitement that was artificially induced by factors beyond the demands of necessity.

The greatest group of Homers ever assembled by one collector was brought together in New York by Thomas B. Clarke. This collection finally numbered sixteen oils and fifteen watercolors, and it included some of Homer's most famous pictures. *The Two Guides, The Carnival, Campfire, The Life Line, Eight Bells, The Lookout — "All's Well," Maine Coast,* and *On the Bright Side* were among the oils. In 1898 Mr. Clarke's collection of paintings by Homer was exhibited with a group of pictures by George Inness at the Union League Club in New York — Mr. Clarke was then chairman of the Club's art committee. This was perhaps a not entirely disinterested move on the part of the collector, for the following year he put his paintings up at auction and received a substantial return on his investment as well as a lot of publicity for his "bravery" in investing in American paintings. The prices established at this sale were of course indirectly valuable to Homer, for besides bringing him to the attention of a wide public it enabled him to raise his prices.

In fact the Clarke sale was one of the most important factors in establishing Homer's reputation among collectors. It really established a new era in collecting and once again made American painting desirable among collectors who had been generally inclined to buy only the work of well-known European artists. It raised the reputations of Homer and George Inness to the point where they were competing on almost equal terms with some of the European painters.

In the early 1890's the newly founded American art museums began to act as patrons of American art, and Homer's pictures became popular with the trustees and directors of these institutions. In 1893 his picture *The Gale* was awarded a gold medal at the World's Columbian Exposition in Chicago, where fifteen of his paintings were shown. His now famous canvas *The Fox Hunt* was purchased in 1894 by the Pennsylvania Academy of Fine Arts in Philadelphia from their annual exhibition. In 1896 his picture *The Wreck* was awarded a gold medal and a cash purchase prize of five thousand dollars by the Carnegie Institute in Pittsburgh. Thus Homer's first gold medals and his largest cash reward up to that time came not from his native Boston but from the supposedly crude and uncultured social frontiers of Illinois and western Pennsylvania. In 1894 the Norcross Fund had given the Boston Museum a painting by Homer — *The Fog Warning* — and the museum purchased another at the Clarke sale: *The Lookout — "All's Well."* At the Paris exposition in 1900 his painting *A Summer Night* was bought for the Luxembourg and he was awarded a gold medal. But the big prizes at the exposition went to Whistler, who by then had practically stopped painting, and to John Singer Sargent, the most dazzling new talent of a younger generation. In 1901 Homer received another gold medal at the Pan-American Exposition in Buffalo for his group of watercolors, and in that same year his *On a Lee Shore* was bought by the Rhode Island School of Design in Providence.

By 1908, when a special group of twenty-two paintings by Homer was put together for display at the Carnegie Annual in Pittsburgh, eleven of them were lent for the occasion by American art museums. It was thought at the time that no other American painter could claim such a distinction. The museums lending to this exhibition were in Boston, Providence, New York, Philadelphia, Washington, and Milwaukee. The remaining eleven paintings in the show all came from private collections.

This was Homer's most important one-man show during his lifetime. Mr. Downes, the art critic of the Boston *Transcript*, had suggested that Homer be given a large exhibition in Boston when plans for a Whistler exhibition fell through (because Whistler refused to co-operate), but strangely enough his suggestion aroused no interest among the art lovers of Boston.

Homer was not a prolific painter — he was not one of those artists who lived to paint, he did not dash off sketches by the hundreds or produce finished canvases by the thousand, as some artists have done. He was not like the British painter Turner, for instance, who at his death left a collection of almost *twenty thousand* watercolors and sketches. Homer painted to live; as long as his pictures sold he was interested in producing them. One of his oldest friends — the artist Joseph Baker — said of Homer: "I do not think that painting was anything more to him than anything else. He did not care whether he painted or not." In the 1890's Homer himself wrote, "at present, and for some time past, I see no reason why I should paint any pictures. . . . I will paint for money any time. Any subject, any size." Remarks of this kind were made by Homer on several occasions and they have been interpreted in various ways, but they would appear to reinforce the idea that he considered his work purely as a business proposition. He made his pictures to sell. Like many British artists of the time he felt that his ideas for subjects and compositions were something to be guarded, like trade secrets, lest they be stolen by some student and put out before his pictures could be finished.

Whatever the cause of these baffling remarks, when we forget them and look at the pictures without reference to the assumed or real attitudes of the painter, they never fail to exert a pleasurable spell that defies explanation. There is in them some indefinable magic, whether of style or subject, that

Metropolitan Museum of Art

MAINE COAST

holds our attention and prints their image upon the memory.

The two paintings *New England Country School* and *Snap the Whip* — both are pictures Homer produced in several varying versions — perhaps contain in themselves just about all that can be said about the simple joys and tribulations of the country schoolboy of 1870 or '80. Though these pictures are concerned with homely subjects, they have about them now an air of innocent rustic charm that seems to represent to modern eyes the very essence of life in the country. These are American pictures that make one grateful for the sympathetic genius who was willing to see in them subjects worthy of his brush. Here one is not conscious of Japanese design or French technique or Ruskinian ideas, though perhaps all these influential ideas were by now well assimilated in the artist's work. Indeed the ideas he absorbed at home and abroad made it possible for him to see the value of such unheroic, perhaps even "inartistic" material. Other subjects of this nature record his search for interesting scenes of rural activities. One reads their titles with a feeling of nostalgia for a way of life that is now gone — *The Nooning; The Country Store; Milking Time; Answering the Horn; Watermelon Boys; Crossing the Pasture;* and so on. Homer's contribution in this area of subject is not unique; other American painters, sometimes following his lead, painted similar subjects, but their pictures do not have the magical hold upon our attention that Homer's paintings never fail to exercise.

In the estimation of some the painting *Promenade on the Beach* is one of Homer's most colorful and charming works. Its unusual color scheme, with its very dark blue sky and brightly lighted sand, gives it an unusual character, such as one expects from Homer — the two young women with their Japanese fans are obviously heroines right out of a novel by William Dean Howells, summering at the shore to escape the sultry rigors of a Boston season.

One painting by Homer that has been rather unjustly neglected shows in the most interesting manner how his study of Japanese prints influenced his color and his compositions. This is *Camp-fire*. The treatment of the figures in their unconventional simplicity is absolutely in the manner of Hokusai. The novel and daring design of the sparks flying up from the fire recalls Japanese prints of fireworks at night — every woodsman has seen fires like this, yet few artists have seized upon this intriguing motive for use as an ornamental element of a composition. The delicate pattern of weeds that lean out of the darkness toward the flames is also Japanese in feeling, yet remains true to nature and to the realistic vision of the American woodsman-artist. The color scheme is one of those bold and successful attacks on an impossible problem — the capture of the color of night, the focus of firelight sunk in the great well of forest darkness. The Japanese elements in this picture are not obvious or forced in any way; the picture is entirely American in subject and feeling. It is here that Homer's genius best reveals itself; in his skillful use of oriental concepts of picturemaking unconfused with picturesque Asiatic externalities.

Viewed from any angle, this painting is a tour de force, a masterpiece that any artist could be proud of; ignore the subject matter and admire the fantastic composition; consider the subtleties of color alone; consider again the picture as an illustration and hear the crackle of the blaze against the nocturnal wilderness silence. Surely this painting must find a place among Homer's best works, and, being there, it must also then stand among the very best American paintings of the time.

One of Homer's most pleasing and most successful pictures is *The Two Guides*, a picture that Kenyon Cox calls "the first" of "his masterpieces." It was painted in 1876, when the artist was forty years old, and it is a matured and measured statement of the artist's full powers. It is a picture that reminds one of Delacroix's comment on a painting by Jacob Jordaens in which he says: "Force, vehemence and splendor free him from the demands of grace and charm," for Homer's painting is strong and splendid in such an individual way that the feebler virtues of grace and charm are not missed. Cox says of this picture that it is "full of the joy of high places and the splendour of fine

CAMPFIRE

weather," and it gives the feeling of the vastness of space that can be found only in mountain meadows and hills that have been "timbered off," as this one has. The composition is a masterpiece of restraint, the two guides stand monumental and right, the very essence of their craft, upon a delicate floral tapestry in the hot light of a summer sun at high noon.

The painting *Hound and Hunter* shows a hound swimming in the water; a man lying prone in a small boat reaches over the bow to grasp the antlers of a swimming deer. This somewhat mysterious subject is a curious document that illustrates the brutal and unsportsmanly method by which hundreds of deer were slaughtered in the Adirondacks in the days before any effort was made to protect the wild life of the forests. A well-known New York sportsman and angler, William C. Prime, who fished the Adirondack waters in the 1860's and '70's describes this kind of a deer hunt as follows: "The Adirondack woods abound in deer. It is an easy matter to kill a half-dozen in a day . . . but I am compelled to say that some Adirondack hunters would not be admitted into the society sportsman hunters . . . for this reason; they butcher the deer here instead of shooting them in a fair way . . . the principal part of the hunting here consists in driving the deer into the lakes, and drowning them in the most abominable manner." This is the subject of our picture, this hunter's dog has started the deer and chased it into the water, the thug in the boat catches the almost helpless animal by the horns and pushes its head under water and holds it there until the unfortunate animal drowns. Our author continues: "This, on my word, is the manner in which nine deer out of ten that are killed in the Adirondacks are murdered."

One of Homer's most powerful hunting pictures is the *Huntsman and Dogs*, belonging to the Philadelphia Museum of Art. From it emanates the savage, desolate atmosphere of mountain country that has been stripped of its forests by loggers. Here we see a tough young backwoods hunter posing in an aggressive stance with a gun, a deer hide slung over his shoulder, and in his hand the antlered head of his kill. Beside him his yelping hounds leap. He stands, proud and forbidding, like a Japanese actor impersonating a samurai, poised before a mountain whose Fujiyama line slopes across the composition like one of those views of the mountain in Hokusai's famous series of the *Thirty-six Views of Fuji*. A cold lead sky completes the frigid and haunting picture.

Metropolitan Museum of Art

SHOWER BEFORE THE MOUNTAIN (Hokusai)

One painting in which the Japanese mode of design is perhaps most conspicuous is the mysterious *Fox Hunt*, in the collection of the Pennsylvania Academy of Fine Arts in Philadelphia. It is said that in deep winter hungry crows have been known to follow a fox making his way with difficulty through heavy snow until he reaches a stage of exhaustion, when the birds can safely attack him. This rather gruesome tale reminds one of the ghostly legends of the Japanese fox demons. The picture can easily be transformed into a perfect Japanese screen by dividing the composition into three vertical panels.

Another canvas in which the Japanese elements of design are particularly strong is the *Searchlight, Harbour Entrance, Santiago de Cuba* painted in 1901. The picture is a subtle study in refined monochrome patterns that were enhanced at the time it was painted by a timely emotional value. The restrained color and the extraordinary composition of his wonderful study *Right and Left*, in the National Gallery in Washington, are so Japanese in style one hesitates to emphasize the point.

The view of *Artist's Studio in a Fog* is one of Homer's most interesting paintings because it shows so clearly the effect of his study of oriental art. In a sense this is an oriental landscape — it is easy to see it as a Sung ink painting, or to see it as a slightly Westernized Japanese print of the kind that was being made in Japan in the 1890's. If this picture had been reproduced by the same wood-block process by which Japanese prints are made, it would need only a few seals and an ideographic signature to complete its oriental character.

At the turn of the century Homer was thought of mainly as a marine painter and his earlier works were considered merely as preparation for these grand sea pieces of his later years. Today the situation is somewhat changed if not completely reversed, and his pictures of everyday life arouse more interest that those abstract visions of stone, surf, and sky that seem to be the most piercingly cruel expressions of desolation and loneliness. These abstract studies of cold gray waves and dark rock under lowering clouds seemed very important aesthetically to the art lovers of 1910, but they are now beginning to appear static and somehow empty. Their content seems to be only what the spectator can put into them by visualizing the artist or some other solitary being hypnotized by the crushing forces that move ceaselessly and restlessly on the shore below, with their terrible and majestic disregard of man, forces unconcerned with any human scale.

There is a curious transition in feeling that separates the early work from the late. In almost all his early works people play an important part in his compositions. But gradually the persistent waters of the sea by erosion seem to have washed away all traces of humanity from his large compositions. They may perhaps symbolize the fearful solitude of man alone in the bitter snow on the shore staring at the very shape of power, deafened with the racking roar of the surf, struggling to stand against the frozen blast of the gale — surely these are paintings of stark brutality and fear.

Perhaps one of the best known of his late marine pictures is *Northeaster*, a large canvas now

Mr. and Mrs. Charles S. Payson

GUIDE CARRYING DEER

in the Metropolitan Museum of Art. It sums up all the things to be found in his other large marine paintings, and in fact it sums up the triumphs and failures of all good marine paintings, for a painting of a wave can only be a static design of flowing liquid, bubbling foam, dashing spray, and the curling breaker, the essence of restless motion, cannot well be represented. Yet some essences of the sea have been caught by Homer, and though these paintings may not be wet and watery, or tossing and splashing, or boiling and surging, one senses in them the weight and power of the rolling breaker and its thunderous shattering on the unyielding rock. Perhaps this aspect of the sea was what interested the artist most; certainly it was what impressed his contemporaries — the powerful tension generated by the opposition of irresistible force meeting immovable body. About a dozen other paintings by Homer are variations upon this theme, and though their titles vary they are usually compositions of only three elements — grim rocks, foaming waves, and stormy skies. Among these might be mentioned: *Cannon Rock* and *The Maine Coast* (both also in the collection of the Metropolitan Museum of Art); *Early Morning after a Storm at Sea,* in the Cleveland Museum of Art; *The Coast in Winter,* in the Worcester Museum; *Stormbeaten; High Cliff, Coast of Maine; Driftwood;* and *Watching the Breakers: A High Sea.*

Dr. and Mrs. S. Emlen Stokes

DRIFTWOOD

The melodramatics of the marine paintings are perhaps principal elements that make the pictures less appealing to modern eyes than those cool nostalgic scenes of everyday life, the life of the farmer, the fisherman, the hunter, and the vacationist, a life that has now vanished, whereas the rocks, sea,

SHARK FISHING

and sky remain unchanged. In Homer's time rural scenes such as he loved to record were a part of the visual memory and experience of practically everyone. This made them seem to sophisticated critics with European-trained tastes to be inartistic, ugly reminders of farm drudgery, and the discomforts of frontier life, while the "artistic" marine studies fitted right in with the advanced critical taste in the artistic circles of the time.

These pictures of the sea are almost exact translations of certain passages in Ruskin's chapter on how water should be represented in a painting. There we read:

> Few people, comparatively, have ever seen the effect on the sea of a powerful gale continued without intermission for three or four days and nights, and to those who have not, I believe it must be unimaginable, not from the mere force or size of surge, but from the complete annihilation of the limit between sea and air . . . imagine the low rain clouds brought down to the very level of the sea . . . whirling and flying in rags and fragments from wave to wave, and finally, conceive the surges themselves in their utmost pitch of power, velocity and vastness and madness, lifting themselves in precipices and peaks, furrowed with their whirl of ascent, through all this chaos . . . there is indeed no distinction left between the sea and air, that no object, nor horizon, nor any landmark or natural evidence of position is left, that the heaven is all spray, and the ocean all cloud. . . .
>
> If . . . whether in a boat, or on some isolated rock . . . on a rocky coast, we abandon ourselves for hours to the passive reception of the great and essential impressions of that which is around us, the only way of arriving at a true feeling of its spirit, the three great ideas which we shall carry away with us will be those of recklessness, power and breadth; — recklessness, manifested in mad, perpetual, changeful undirected motion; not of wave after wave, as it appears from the shore, but of the

very same water rising and falling . . . it is when we perceive that it is . . . the same water, constantly rising and crashing and recoiling, and rolling in again in new forms and with fresh fury, that we perceive the perturbed spirit and feel the intensity of its unwearied rage. The sensation of power is also trebled for not only is the vastness of apparent size much increased, but the whole action is different; it is not a passive wave rolling sleepily forward until it tumbles heavily, prostrated upon the beach, but a sweeping exertion of tremendous and living strength, which does not now appear to fall but to burst upon the shore, which never perishes, but recoils and recovers. Finally the sensation of breadth is peculiarly impressed, not by the extent of the sea itself, but by the enormous sweep and hollow of every wave . . . and by the grand unity of the curves of the breakers. . . .

And again:

Of the color of this magnificent sea I have before spoken, it is a solemn green grey, with its foam seen dimly through the darkness of twilight, modulated with the fulness, changefulness, and sadness of a deep wild melody.

Though Homer's studies of wave patterns finally became almost complete abstractions, one sees in them — and in all his paintings of water — echos of these descriptions by Ruskin as well as the force and curling grandeur of Hokusai's *Great Wave*. It was of course from this famous print that Homer took his idea for the startling composition called *Kissing the Moon*, where only a fragment of a suggestion of the gunwale of a dory buoys up three men deep in a trough of waves. Such strange and

Metropolitan Museum of Art

THE GREAT WAVE OFF KANAGAWA (Hokusai)

KISSING THE MOON

unconventional compositional devices as this gave his work its unconventional and very compelling attraction — qualities he shared with few other American artists of his time.

Homer's greatest picture, *The Gulf Stream*, moved the critic Sadakichi Hartmann to write in his history of American art: "Today his vision is as fresh and unconventional and his power and individuality as indisputable as ever. His *In the Gulf Stream* . . . is one of the greatest pictures ever painted in America."

These are strong words, but time seems to have backed up the judgment of the critic. In any case there can be little doubt that this painting has retained its powerful fascination, and it remains popular year after year with museum visitors and with color-print buyers. It is one of his few important large oil paintings that were developed from sketches made in the Bahamas, and it may very well be the most important picture he ever painted. Certainly it is one that presents the peculiar talents of the artist at their very best. The choice of such an unusual subject is one of the hallmarks of Homer's work, and here he seems to have selected a particularly enigmatic and tantalizing episode, a marine puzzle that floats forever in a region of unsolved mysteries, for this is frankly a storytelling picture — perhaps one should call it a story-suggesting picture, for the artist leaves the construction of the story to the spectator.

But aside from these compelling literary qualities, if they may be so-called, the picture is a triumph on other grounds, on purely artistic grounds, for it is a handsome and subtle composition, one that repays close study; its color is unusually pleasing. It is a picture that might seem to have a few oriental characteristics, yet their refining and strengthening touch may perhaps be detected in the stylization of the strokes, which make the pattern of wavelets; these characteristics can be traced in the lifting cant of the hulk, in the relation of the curved gunwales to the boundaries of the picture field, as well as in the detached point of view of the spectator.

Some of the original watercolor studies for this subject were made in Nassau as early as 1885, but the theme was not developed on canvas until 1899. The picture was exhibited in an unfinished state at the Pennsylvania Academy of Fine Arts in Philadelphia in 1900. After this showing Homer made a number of improvements on the painting and sent it to his dealer, priced at $4000. For a time, strangely enough, the picture attracted little attention. The Worcester Museum considered buying it, but the subject matter was finally judged to be too unpleasant, too brutal for the sensitive art lovers of central Massachusetts in 1902. In 1906 the canvas was sent to the winter exhibition of the National Academy of Design in New York, an exhibition that was held then in the galleries of the Fine Arts Building on West Fifty-seventh Street (the home of the Art Students League). According to the account in *American Art News*, when the picture was brought before the gentlemen of the jury, someone was heard to say, "Boys, that ought to be in the Metropolitan." A petition suggesting that the museum buy the painting was drawn up then and there and signed by all the members of the jury — Kenyon Cox, the artist and author, was the chairman of the jury — the petition was forwarded with a letter to Robert W. de Forest, secretary of the museum, from Will H. Low. After due deliberation the trustees of the museum decided to follow the suggestion of the artists and the painting was bought. Roger Fry, who was then curator of paintings at the museum, wrote to the Academy Committee to convey the news that the museum was going to carry out their suggestion, saying:

> To my great delight it was agreed to purchase the picture . . . I need not tell you how delighted I am personally. I regard The Gulf Stream as one of the most typical and central creations of American art . . . It is a great masterpiece and counts among the very finest that Winslow Homer has created.

A note published in the Museum's *Bulletin* by Bryson Burroughs in January 1907 describes the painting and remarks that "the *Gulf Stream* would be ranked among his figure subjects, and no other work of his could better show his power in this direction . . . This is a story-telling picture, and the story assumes the proportions of a great allegory if one chooses. If not, the rendering of the sea, and the sharks, the sunlit hulk, and the splendid figure, will suffice for the acceptance of the *Gulf Stream* as one of the master works of contemporary art. The Museum is fortunate in securing this picture, and its acknowledgments are due to the Jury . . . of the Academy Exhibition, at whose suggestion the purchase was made."

The newspaper accounts of the academy exhibition contain interesting information about the painting and interesting side lights on contemporary art criticism. Perhaps the most entertaining one is from the New York *Press* of December 23, 1906. *The Gulf Stream* "is head and shoulders over everything in the rooms . . . Winslow Homer's composition has the distinction in addition to its merits as a piece of wonderful craftsmanship and its tragic story, of being the first canvas that was ever purchased by the Metropolitan Museum at an Academy show. It is a marine and depicts a small sloop that has been dismasted by a tropical squall . . . Pictorially this is all striking enough, but technically the painting is even more remarkable. The introduction of the note of brilliant red in the foreground, on the rail of the sloop [actually it is on the water line] is a masterly stroke that kept a crowd of artists before the canvas all day long on Friday in open admiration of Homer's genius for color."

Among Homer's paintings of the sea one of the most famous is *The Life Line*. Perhaps no other marine painting combines so effectively the dramatic aspects of rescue with the enigmatic elements of design, vitalizing this subject with sensations that prevent the drama from sinking into melodrama and the enigmas from descending to childish puzzles. Critics have always remarked in this picture the unusual device of the hidden face of the man who rescues the shipwreck victim. This convention, however strange it may seem to the Western observer, is a commonplace in Japanese prints that illustrate romantic novels where pairs of hopeless lovers, in the act of committing suicide by jumping into the sea, are always represented entwined in such an embrace and with flying drapery covering their faces.

At the time *The Life Line* was painted (it was exhibited at the National Academy of Design in 1884) the terrors of shipwreck were much more common than they are now, and sailors could often depend only on dead reckoning or on instinct to gauge winds and calculate drift or on subtle changes in the color of the water to locate reefs and shoals. In those days there were many more small ships plying along the coast than there are now, and the lifesaving stations (first established in Tynemouth, England, in 1864) were a recent innovation on the American coast. At that time tales of danger and heroism at sea and the daring rescues made by lifesaving crews were vital topics in every seaport.

In Homer's time the harbor of Tynemouth had among seamen a fame unenvied as the scene of frequent and spectacular shipwrecks. But balancing this baleful reputation was the bright fame of its lifesaving crews, made up of volunteers from its population of fishermen and sailors. Their heroism and success finally brought about the regular organization of a series of lifesaving stations along the English coast, and their fame was world-wide. Perhaps the fame of Tynemouth as both the scene of

Corcoran Gallery of Art

LIGHT ON THE SEA

shipwrecks and as the seat of the lifesaving service, as well as its reputation among artists for its picturesque fishermen and their fishwives, their boats and nets, their sturdy simple lives, all attracted Homer, who sought dramatic marine subjects for his large paintings and found there endless material for sketches.

The Lookout — "All's Well" and the painting titled *Eight Bells* are such essential statements of their subjects they seem in themselves to sum up completely the salt and substance of the mariner's life. The men in these pictures, performing their required tasks, immediately engage our confidence in their competence to deal effectively with any situation the treachery or violence of the sea may produce.

In paintings like *The Herring Net, The Fog Warning,* and *Lost on the Grand Banks* we have an accurate record of the hard and dangerous life of the deep-sea fishermen touched here by the artist with melancholy overtones of tragedy and loneliness.

Homer's paintings in watercolor fall into two distinct groups according to their style and date. In the 1880's his style changed from the rather careful tinted drawing — the traditional British style of watercolor — to the free, broad, direct painting with large brushes loaded with pure color. This transition was one that Homer and many artists before him have made as they came to feel more and more at ease in handling this difficult medium. The change in Homer's style was perhaps more conspicuous because so few American watercolor painters in his time ever got very far beyond the tinted-drawing stage.

Homer's early watercolors appear to have some of the same characteristics, as far as technique goes, as the work of the famous British watercolor painter David Cox (1783–1859). The color is cool and reserved, laid on in thin washes, the handling is prim, gentle, and correct, almost ladylike in fact. But in the later watercolors these characteristics are soon lost in his steadily advancing adventurousness and freedom in both color and brushwork. At last in the 1890's and in the final decade of his life his hand had attained its ultimate degree of skill, which gave to the works of those years their magnificent free-flowing perfection.

Homer's paintings seem to be predominantly cerebral rather than emotional, they are thoughts expressed as pictures, they are a recording of facts, a recounting of a story, perhaps, told in pictorial form; but they are told without sentimentality. That Homer felt strongly about the subjects of his pictures cannot be doubted, but though his feelings were deep and strong, they were never empurpled with intense romantic passion or hazy poetic emotionalism. His pictures appear to be studied with a cool intellectual detachment even when his brush moves with the swift bravura that characterizes his later watercolor paintings. This detachment is perhaps a characteristic of the New England mind, one that leads in one direction to rugged independence and in the other to a rather cold isolation, a barrier against the display of much simple human warmth or passion. In any case it is one of Homer's principal virtues, yet in this virtue is contained the seed of what is perhaps Homer's only serious fault — an impersonal coolness and detachment.

GIRLS WITH LOBSTER

Metropolitan Museum of Art

SLOOP, BERMUDA

HUNTSMAN AND DOGS

THE GULF STREAM

CHAPTER NINE

SUMMING UP

*"A taste for the beautiful is most cultivated out of doors where there is
no house and no housekeeper."*

THOREAU, *Walden*

WINSLOW HOMER has achieved the kind of lasting fame that few other American artists of the
nineteenth century have won. Interest in his work has not slackened in the years since his death.
In fact during this usually critical period, when the reputations of most artists sink rapidly into the
backwaters of biographical dictionaries, the reputation of Homer seems to have always been on the
increase. He has managed to maintain a high reputation among critics and art historians, and public
enthusiasm for his work has remained lively. Perhaps this is the real test of Homer's powers as a
painter — that he continues to hold and attract the favorable attention of several disparate generations of admirers and enthusiasts. It is a test, one might say, that Homer has passed with flying colors.

In his later years Homer made an almost complete withdrawal from casual social contacts. To
many people it seemed inexcusable that "the greatest American painter" should prefer to devote himself exclusively to painting, hunting, fishing, and gardening; to the basic essentials of life as he saw it.
He had no time for importunate visitors, notoriety seekers or professional art lovers, he never wanted
to teach young ladies to paint, and he refused to co-operate with lion hunters and social climbers. In
this he was not necessarily anti-social, he merely loved his privacy more than their company.

In a magazine article Kenyon Cox wrote of Homer: "He was always making the most unexpected
observations and painting things that were not only unpainted till then, but, apparently unseen by
anyone else." Certainly the kind of thing seen and painted by Homer was quite unseen by many
American painters, including Kenyon Cox himself, but on the other hand the kind of thing that Homer
saw and painted was not overlooked entirely by such American artists as Mary Cassatt, or even
Whistler; French artists like Manet, Degas, Van Gogh, and Gauguin all had this special ability of
seeing; and of course countless Japanese print makers and thousands of oriental artists before them
all had this mysterious gift of being able to see things generally unseen and the skill to paint them with
vitality and individual style.

Some people have been disturbed by Homer's common-sense commercial attitude toward his
work. He very rightly considered his pictures as valuable products, made with all the painstaking
care that a conscientious and well-trained artist naturally puts into his work; this is what the artist
sells — the product of his art. To Homer the making and selling of a picture were a part of the everyday business of earning a living; it was not considered by him as a mysterious aesthetic experience.
When his pictures didn't sell, Homer felt himself to be an unsuccessful businessman, but it is impossible to imagine him thinking of himself as a misunderstod genius. Near the end of his life this commercial attitude toward his work became more and more pronounced until it verged on an exclusive

interest in money. Some of his threats to stop painting altogether were based on the fact that he had earned enough money to support himself comfortably without working.

Some critics have said that Homer was merely a recorder of storytelling pictures, and some of them, it is true, do have elements of pictorial narrative; but in spite of this no one could possibly consider Homer as a mere "literary" painter, as one who depended on an author for his ideas. Homer's pictures present scenes that suggest certain trains of thought, but he does not make up illustrations to tales already told. His "stories," if we may call them that, are sources of thought rather than the complementary visualization of the written word. The subjects of his pictures are developments from general themes and ideas, not the pictorial elaboration of anecdotes. They are provocative; they make the viewer produce his own version of a new story based on elements that Homer has selected and presented. This kind of achievement in art is a rare one, and in Homer's time there were few American painters who could even begin to approach his talent for this special kind of storytelling.

In view of this it is somewhat surprising to find one modern critic dismissing Homer with the comment that he had an eye only for surfaces and happy snapshots of outdoor life. This must surely be an unpopular point of view, because most spectators find in Homer's pictures some special personal quality he put into them that quite enlivens and transforms the "surface" and "snapshot" aspects of his work, a mysterious quality that vivifies and permeates even some of his frankly journalistic reports, something that makes even these into pictures of lasting interest.

There is about his work none of the stale air of foreign ateliers, and still less of the tepid provincial manners found in most of the home studios of New York or Boston, where the air was thick with

Metropolitan Museum of Art

MOONLIGHT—WOOD'S ISLAND LIGHT

aesthetic clichés and where some artists consciously assumed romantically artistic poses. From Homer's pictures flows fresh and free the sparkling-clear memory of out-of-doors America interpreted with individual power and style. His pictures recall the cool black silence of the deep woods, the aromatic scent of pine and fir when the hot sun of August burns the noon air. One hears in them the terrible, lonely, heart-stopping cry of the desolate loon echoing over the darkling waters of some lost mountain pond. At other times they convey the breath of salt air of the rough Maine shore, the seeping fogs, the sinister rocks wet with the astringent spray of the ceaselessly pounding sea. Sometimes they flash with the coruscating brilliance of hot Caribbean isles, lush and soft, washed in blue waters, waters that are often spiked with the accents of tropical danger or violence — the hurricane cloud, the waterspout, or the sliding menace of shark.

One of Homer's greatest talents and one that gave his paintings their most easily grasped characteristic was his gift for plain old-fashioned sincerity (a Pre-Raphaelite virtue). For when we study his pictures we feel that the artist offers us, not some optical trickery, some painterly sleight-of-hand, some prestidigitator's illusion calculated to bemuse, but simply the plain Ruskinian truths he saw before him. These facts, however, are never presented in a commonplace way; they are usually seen from some new angle, perhaps, or patterned in a way that only Homer would have used. The planned organization of his pictures is there to be analyzed by those who care to do so, but it never interferes with the simple clarity of statement that is such an important aspect of his sincerity. Whether he speaks to us of the sea and shore, the forest and the farm, the language and accent are always the plain, terse, everyday speech of New England conveying the plain, everyday home truths. This simplicity, this sincerity, this lack of consciously artistic embellishments, is perhaps one of the most potent sources of the nostalgic power his paintings now generate, for these scenes, of rural serenity, of

Alastair B. Martin

CAPE TRINITY, SAGUENAY RIVER

NASSAU

NATURAL BRIDGE, NASSAU

SHORE AND SURF, NASSAU

FISHING BOATS, KEY WEST

the vast and dangerous freedoms of the mountains and of the sea, now appear to offer to us vistas back into what we think of as a simpler and possibly more wholesome day and way of living, where hard labor and danger provided rewards and stimulation, where the strength of man was pitted against the forces of nature. There one finds the wilderness guide with only an ax and rifle to depend on; there is the deep-sea fisherman in his small, frail dory, calm in his knowledge of winds and tides, or the farmer sweat-stained, hard-handed, yet confident.

One might consider Homer as one of the New England poets, although he was a poet whose verses were to be painted and not printed. His poetry, however, is not of a literary kind, he is not concerned with the sophisticated mechanics of the sonnet, his poetry is not voiced in the polite and measured cadences of the drawing room, but it is set forth in strong rhythmic patterns, simple and natural in the melodious manner of the folksong, the sea chantey or the camp-meeting hymn. As a poet he would be closer to the plain Quakerisms of Whittier than to the scholarly urbanities of Longfellow or the deeper philosophical thoughts of Emerson.

In order to understand Homer the man it is necessary to recall that, though he lived a rather simple life in his New York studio and in his retreat on the coast of Maine, it is not to be supposed that he did not enjoy his little luxuries, especially after his financial success as a painter allowed him to indulge his tastes. He loved his after-dinner cigars, his bracers of old scotch whisky, and the cases of tinned delicacies shipped down to Prouts Neck from S. S. Pierce's in Boston. He was no ascetic hermit starving to death for his art.

It is well to remember that, although Homer earned his living as an illustrator and as a painter for over fifty years, he was always at heart a sportsman who had from early youth loved the magical freedoms and exhilaration of the out-of-door life. He knew the splendor of the forest and field, the satisfactions of the successful hunter and fisherman. He knew the rough amenities of the woodsman's shack and the open campfire where the aroma of bacon and fresh-caught trout and coffee boiled up in a tin can surpassed anything that Paris had to offer in the way of food. He knew the magnificent solitude and silence of the drifting canoe. These were things he found to be irresistible, and their effect on his work as an artist was very great. There were many other American artists of the time who were also fishermen, hunters, woodsmen who knew their way about in the wilderness; others were competent sailors who knew the ways of the sea and sail, yet somehow the paintings of these men, interesting as they may be, cannot compare with the visions of the wilderness and the sea that Homer recorded.

There were artists of the time who knew much more of the Indian arts of woodcraft and the secrets of the wilderness guides and scouts than Homer ever knew, but he brought to the wilderness a kind of trained and sophisticated vision, a free, native skill of hand that the other men seemed to lack. Some American artists when they went to Paris to study were so oppressed by the city they abandoned their studies and fled west at the first opportunity to the safety of the home prairies and forests. One of these was the sculptor and illustrator Edward Kemeys, a man who lived and thought like an Indian and signed his works with the totem mark of the wolf head.

Homer, a hunter at home in the woods and fields, was equally at home under sail and knew how to manage a small boat. These were the things that delighted him, and by his skill with the brush he was able for the greater part of his life to enjoy these pleasures to the full. This is perhaps the true measure of his success, that he found a way to do pretty much what he wanted to with a minimum of hard labor. Though planning a picture may be considered complicated, perhaps even difficult work, it was really a task far closer to pleasure than to the kind of day-to-day drudgery that marks the lives of most people. Homer's life and work were powerfully influenced by his love of the freedom of the forest wilderness that still pressed close upon many American cities in his time, and its effect is visible

HURRICANE, BAHAMAS

in his work as it is in all the American ways of thinking and doing in our literature and art.

James Flexner has said that "Homer's images strike the eye with the vitality of a woodsman's axe." The word play might indeed be carried further without straining the point, for in truth the brush handle seems to lie in the hand of the artist easily and naturally with that same smooth fitness and rightness that makes the ax helve lie at home in the grasp of the born woodsman. Homer was both an American woodsman and an American artist and his talents as a painter came to him as naturally as his talents for life in the woods, his skill with rod and trout fly, with ax, gun, and trap. He knew how to direct these native skills as a woodsman and his instincts as an artist led him safely around the artistic deadfalls and artistic trivialities to the real thing in just the same way that a born woodsman can follow an unblazed trail through a wilderness to a rendezvous in unmapped territory.

It is not logical to suppose that Winslow Homer was not, in childhood and youth, made aware of the things of the mind. Since he was brought up in a proper Boston family in the scholarly and intellectual atmosphere of Cambridge, he could scarcely have escaped from these subtle and powerful influences, for after all, life in Cambridge when Homer was growing up was centered upon the college, the pulpit, the lecture hall, and the library. In any home, no matter how humble, one could discuss Emerson's current lectures or read Mr. Thoreau's new book *Walden, or Life in the Woods*. In fact judging from Homer's paintings as well as from his scattered remarks and his way of life it is almost certain that he knew and absorbed Thoreau's and Emerson's writings on solitude, on self-reliance, and on the conduct of life. One feels not only that these men, with Ruskin, were familiar reading to him but that their teachings formed in no small degree the basis of his conduct as a man and as an artist. Many of Homer's paintings seem to celebrate the same intense feeling for wild nature that one finds in the writings of Thoreau, and many of Homer's odd notions fit into the tough-minded Yankee pattern so plainly revealed in Thoreau's writings. If Thoreau is "the most American writer and thinker of his time," it is possible that Homer, following in his own obtuse and independent way, the steps of the Concord philosopher, came naturally to his own high place as "the most American painter of his time."

Probably Homer went to Prouts Neck to live for the same reason that Thoreau went to live at Walden Pond, "not to live cheaply nor to live dearly there, but to transact some private business with the fewest obstacles; to be hindered from accomplishing which for want of a little common sense, a little enterprise and business talent, appeared not so sad as foolish."

In Homer's best work one senses the cool and sure directing and organizing power of a distinguished and unusual mentality. His pictures reveal the serene and free intellectuality of the artist's mind; they are not fervent emotional statements dashed off in a cloud of romantic agony. They disclose his rare sense of detachment; his vision is clear, steady, and purposeful. He never saw a landscape through a veil of mystical and poetic tears like Inness did. His pictures are not "suggestions" or "arrangements" of unsubstantial patches of muted grays and browns like some of Whistler's rather vaporous if not completely formless studies. Homer was not a romantic dreamer, he was always the accurate reporter, the scientific observer. To him a landscape was perhaps a series of plain physical and geographical facts, but they are facts his eye interpreted in striking pictorial patterns calculated

Museum of Fine Arts, Boston

LEAPING TROUT

WILD GEESE

for visual impact, and both fact and pattern are always considered with placid detachment and aloofness, with all emotions held firmly in check. Inness saw his landscapes as eulogies to the glory of God; Inness himself was emotionally involved with his own beautiful expression of his appreciation of the beauties of nature. Homer stands aside, much more like a stage manager, calmly directing the action and pattern of people and things, molding and shading his picture to the point where its meaning is most forcefully and rightly told.

Homer's figures have solidity, weight, mass; they stand firmly; they are always correctly balanced and their gesture and stance are always knowingly expressed and set down without hesitation. Yet, having all these important qualities of draftsmanship, they seem to possess no anatomical structure; there is no warm flesh articulating a bony structure beneath the garments. These figures are impersonal volumes, male and female forms recognizable by silhouette and costume as men and women; but they are human shapes without viscera, without warmth, yet strangely enough, though they lack this important quality, they all seem to have vitality, they are alive. His few half-nude figures are completely unvoluptuous and without any shade of sensuality. This curiously impersonal view of humanity is also a marked characteristic of Homer's heads and faces. Studying them, one feels that with a very few random exceptions — for instance a few of the faces of his Negro subjects — these faces are never portraits. The women are cold, straight-nosed Pre-Raphaelite beauties with impassive expressions like those of the sculptured goddesses one sees on courthouses, or like the vapid ladies whose faces one finds in old-fashioned drawing books. The faces of his men are equally impassive, impersonal, and interchangeable. In fact almost all of these people in face and figure are mere types; they seldom rise to the individuality of particular persons. Perhaps this general impersonality of faces and bodies is a reflection of Homer's desire not to become involved with other people, the desire which eventually made him into the crusty recluse of Prouts Neck. Homer the artist saw his men and women not as human beings but as elements of design — they are patterns, volumes, masses, gestures. Homer the proper Boston man primly ignores the warm flesh and the pulsing blood.

Being a New Englander, with a practical point of view, he chose subjects always firmly controlled by intellectual purpose; it was not a purely aesthetic selection prompted at hazard by emotional vagaries. His pictures are based in ideas rather than in the painterly problems that so conspicuously occupied the eyes and brushes of so many of his contemporaries. This is perhaps another key to his enduring fame, for the unchanging basis of human interests and ideas remains constant from century to century, while the aesthetic enthusiams of one generation or of one school of artists can fall from popular favor almost overnight and become worse than outmoded, a subject of mirth and object of mockery.

Mrs. Van Rensselaer in her interesting essay on Winslow Homer says: "The great value of America to the painter is that it is full of new things to be done." Few American painters of the late nineteenth century seem to have fully realized their opportunity to see new things in a new way as Homer did. Most of them were content, as we have noted, to see the new American scenes through the

Worcester Art Museum

RUM CAY

THE BATHER

borrowed lenses of various European styles of painting; the explicit but dead realism of Düsseldorf; the dark brown style of the Munich school; the boudoir and candy-box style of the French Salon, the misty, poetic style of Corot and the Barbizon school, all of these more or less faithfully copied and usually weakened in the copying. When American paintings were exhibited in Europe, the foreign critics were not slow to point out this damning fact until they came to the work of Homer, who usually won the distinction of their approval for his truly individual American way of painting and seeing.

It was to his friend J. Foxcroft Cole that Homer made his famous Ruskinian remark about not looking at pictures if one wishes to be a great artist. It has somewhat baffled people since. Perhaps it can be laid to pure youthful bravado and high spirits; to a playful desire to shock and amuse. It is a statement that by its patent absurdity startles the listener into serious thought. However, in any case, this apophthegm has in it the seed of Homer's way of thinking about his art. It appears to mean that if one aspires to be a great artist one should look at life or look into his own heart rather than merely to study paintings. This interpretation would at least seem logical if it is applied to Homer's own work.

It is the mark of his unerring instinct as an artist, his imaginative flexibility, that from the first, when presented with the utterly foreign art of the Japanese print, Homer was able to recognize its incomparable mastery of design and, furthermore, to realize its immediate value to the development of his own work. He knew a good thing when he saw it, and, like any good Yankee, he set about adapting this good thing to his own purposes. Perhaps his immediate sensing of a kinship with these oriental masters was the result of a long-standing receptiveness of the New England mind to the philosophical ideas and arts of the Orient, intangible treasures that came to Massachusetts with the cargoes of China tea and spices and silks, not to mention the pottery from Canton and Nanking and the black-and-gold lacquer boxes that imperceptibly had introduced into the Western imagination some of the ideas and motives of oriental landscape painting. The mark of Homer's true genius was his ability to assimilate the new ideas presented by Japanese prints — a totally new way of thinking about his own craft — so skillfully and so subtly that the larger principles of design, and of color, and of composition, which animate and form the art of ukiyoye, became the guiding principles upon which he could plan paintings that have secured his fame.

One of the very best aspects of Winslow Homer's work is that it is the reflection of his inventive individuality. He restores one's faith in man as a creative artist. His pictures refresh the eye with their original design and color; his choice of subject and his point of view are always unique; what he borrows he controls; his adaptations from foreign art, whether they come from the Orient or from Europe, remain always subordinate to his own personal style. His masterly skill in selecting and adapting the useful essence of the Japanese print maker's style without getting entangled in obvious copying of surface detail or the self-conscious *japonerie* that Whistler affected, is perhaps the true measure of Homer's greatness as an American painter.

In his own time the critics and writers on art all considered Homer as a marine painter. His earlier paintings of everyday life on the farm such as he produced at the beginning of his career were deliberately overlooked or considered merely as incidental and somewhat trivial preparations for his discovery of his true métier as a painter of the sea. However, his progress from scenes of daily life in the country to the abstract studies of waves and rocks, studies wherein the overwhelming force of the living waters of the sea collide in thunderous tumult against the silent, inert stone of a frozen cliff, reflects the artist's keen though perhaps unconscious or instinctive apperception of certain aspects of the dominant thought or time-spirit of his day. For these dominant elements affected the work of all the writers and artists of the time to just that degree in which they were sensitive to what was going on around them. In this respect Homer's choice of subject throughout his career reveals an interesting if little considered aspect of his work.

The subjects of his earlier pictures, as we have noted, are almost without exception connected with vacation-time activities — times when the realities of existence are for the moment ignored in the make-believe ideal existence of the summer resort, the summer boarding at the farm, the traveling in the byways of the South, or the camp life of the vacationing hunter or fisherman. The real subject of these pictures is the escape from the tensions and troubles of modern life in the city. One of the most important sources of that nostalgic charm we feel so strongly in his work is that these subjects depicting the simplicities of rural life with its mild amusements — the berry picking, the corn husking, apple bees, the gossip at the general store, the boys and girls in school, and all the rest, the Adirondack guides, the Negroes in Virginia just after the Civil War — every one of these subjects is representative of phases of American life that were just about to disappear before the new powers and new attitudes of mind that marked so strongly the closing decades of the nineteenth century. Their subjects not only represent an escape from the grim realities of life in 1870 or 1880, but, it is to be noted, they are all, in their way, pictures of places and people who existed in cultural or social backwaters completely separated from the main currents of life.

On the other hand, the late paintings of the sea — particularly the ones without figures — are really abstractions expressing stark and inhuman elemental forces unsoftened with any reference to man. These paintings of abstract power may be said to reflect the artist's reaction to the worship of absolute power, which was one of the dominant characteristics of American thought and life in his time. This was probably one of the reasons that his pictures appealed so strongly to powerful business-

WOMAN ON A BEACH (tile)

THE MINK POND

men who unconsciously saw in them reflections of their own pleasure in the sense of power.

Though Homer was always an independent artist with a strong individual style of his own, he nevertheless was subject — as all artists are — to various external influences that he molded into a unified personal style unmistakably his. He was unlike many of the artists of his time in that he never lost or deserted his own style to become an imitator. Though his early training was all in the traditional British manner, he never slavishly copied the style of Turner or Ruskin, Burne-Jones, Rossetti, or Landseer, or Millais. After his trip to Paris he did not work in the style of Manet, Courbet, Velazquez, or Hokusai. His vision was never diverted by any scientific theories like those of the French impressionists, nor was it blurred in mist as an instinctive retaliatory stroke against the hard, mechanical realism of the photograph.

Homer's introduction to Japanese prints — whether he saw them first in Boston or New York or in Paris is of little moment — his study of Ruskin, and his introduction to the bold modern work of British and French artists in 1867 provided him with a philosophy, a way of thinking and feeling about painting, a special way of seeing, that sustained and enlivened his imagination for the rest of his life. These European and oriental influences, so deftly absorbed into his basic Anglo-American traditional manner, the manner of the British illustrator and the painter in watercolor, were the materials from which his peculiar genius selected and blended elements that ultimately formed him as an artist. Perhaps his indifference to the critics and to the work of his fellow American painters was only an outward expression of his independent and solitary progress to his own personal style, a style that by his subtle synthesis evolved from many converging impulses into something uniquely his that appeared to his contemporaries, as it does to us today, as one of the finest expressions of the American spirit.

In closing, perhaps it would not be amiss to quote from the inscription of a memorial print honoring Hiroshige, for the words apply with equal grace and appropriateness to Winslow Homer: "He studied hard by himself, and had often to climb mountains and descend to valleys, in order to sketch from nature."

Cooper Union Museum

SNAP THE WHIP

BIBLIOGRAPHY

There are only a few books devoted to Winslow Homer. The most important ones are:

1. William Howe Downes — *The Life and Works of Winslow Homer*. 1911.
   Although this book has the distinction of being the first general work on Homer, and the author had the benefit of advice from Homer's family, the book is an old-fashioned work, a plodding compilation of facts and quotations, yet it remains an important source of information about the artist.

2. Kenyon Cox — *Winslow Homer*. 1914.
   Cox was a painter and his essay discusses Homer's work from the point of view of a rather conventional-minded fellow artist.

3. Forbes Watson — *Winslow Homer*. 1942.
   This is essentially a picture book with a brief introductory text based on Downes.

4. Lloyd Goodrich — *Winslow Homer*. 1944.
   A detailed biographical study — the standard work on the artist's life. The book is of especial interest for its quotations from Homer's letters. It contains a large selection of black-and-white illustrations and an exhaustive bibliography. Unfortunately this book is now out of print.

5. Lloyd Goodrich — *Winslow Homer*. Great American Artists Series. 1959.
   A picture book with an introductory essay revised and expanded from a text originally written for the Metropolitan Miniature Series. Bibliography.

Naturally the work of Winslow Homer is discussed in all the books dealing with the history of American painting. Among the principal works of this sort are:

1. Samuel Isham — *History of American Painting*. 1905.
2. Suzanne LaFollette — *Art in America*. 1929.
3. Oliver Larkin — *Art and Life in America*. 1949.
4. Virgil Barker — *American Painting*. 1950.
5. James Flexner — *Pocket History of American Painting*. 1950.
6. Edgar Richardson — *Painting in America*. 1956.

PRESIDENT LINCOLN, GENERAL GRANT AND TAD LINCOLN

CHRONOLOGY

1836—born in Boston, February 24.

1842—age 6—The Homer family moved to Cambridge about this time.

1846—age 10—Cambridge.

1854—age 18—Cambridge; entered the lithography shop of J. H. Bufford in Boston as an apprentice.

1856—age 20—Cambridge.
　　Book illustration: in "Proceedings at the Reception and Dinner in Honor of George Peabody," Boston, 1856.

1857—age 21—Boston; quit Bufford's and set up as a free-lance illustrator.
　　Illustrations: in *Ballou's Pictorial* and *Harper's Weekly*.

1858—age 22—Boston.
　　Illustrations: in *Ballou's Pictorial* and *Harper's Weekly*.

1859—age 23—Boston, New York; moved to latter in fall, lived at 52 East Sixteenth St., had a studio on Nassau St.
　　Illustrations: in *Ballou's Pictorial* and *Harper's Weekly*.
　　Book illustrations: in Eddy's *The Percy Family*.

1860—age 24—New York; attended drawing class in Brooklyn.
　　Illustrations: in *Harper's Weekly*.
　　Exhibited: New York, National Academy of Design:

SKATING IN CENTRAL PARK

1861—age 25—New York; moved to studio in New York University Building, Washington Square; summer, near Boston; fall, in
　　　　Virginia with Army of the Potomac; instructed in oil-painting technique by Frédéric Rondel.
　　Illustrations: in *Harper's Weekly*.

1862—age 26—New York; spring in Virginia on Peninsular Campaign.
　　Illustrations: in *Harper's Weekly*.
　　　　Painting:　　　　THE SHARPSHOOTER

1863—age 27—New York; occasional trips to Virginia.
　　Illustrations: in *Harper's Weekly*.
　　Exhibited: New York, National Academy of Design:

LAST GOOSE AT YORKTOWN
HOME SWEET HOME

1864—age 28—New York; elected an associate of the National Academy of Design.
　　Illustrations: in *Harper's Weekly*.
　　Exhibited: New York, National Academy of Design:

IN FRONT OF THE GUARD HOUSE
THE BRIERWOOD PIPE

1865—age 29—New York; elected a National Academician.
　　Illustrations: in *Harper's Weekly; Frank Leslie's Chimney Corner*.
　　Exhibited: New York, National Academy of Design:

ZOUAVES PITCHING QUOITS
THE BRIGHT SIDE
THE INITIALS

1866—age 30—New York; in late fall departed for France.
　　Illustrations: in *Frank Leslie's Illustrated Newspaper: Our Young Folks*.
　　Book illustrations: in Cooke: *Surry of Eagle's Nest*; Saunders *Festival of Song*; Tennyson: *Gems from Tennyson*.
　　Exhibited: New York, National Academy of Design:

THE BRUSH HARROW
PRISONERS FROM THE FRONT

1867—age 31—Paris; in late fall departed for New York.
    Illustrations: in *Harper's Weekly*; *Frank Leslie's Illustrated Newspaper: Our Young Folks*; *Riverside Magazine*.
    Book illustration: in Gordon's *Our Fresh and Salt Tutors*.
    Exhibited: Paris exposition:

                    PRISONERS FROM THE FRONT
                    THE BRIGHT SIDE

    Brooklyn Art Association:

                    THE INITIALS

    New York, American Water Color Society

1868—age 32—New York; summer in White Mountains.
    Illustrations: in *Harper's Weekly*; *The Galaxy*; *Our Young Folks*.
    Book illustrations: in *Good Stories*, Part III.
    Exhibited: New York, National Academy of Design:

                    PICARDIE, FRANCE
                    THE STUDIO

    Brooklyn Art Association:

                    FRENCH PASTORAL
                    SPRING VIOLETS

1869—age 33—New York; summer in White Mountains.
    Illustrations: in *Harper's Weekly*; *Appleton's Journal*; *The Galaxy*; *Harper's Bazaar*; *Hearth & Home*; *Our Young Folks*.
    Book illustrations: in Barnes: *Rural Poems*; Edwards: *Susan Fielding*.
    Exhibited: New York, National Academy of Design:

                    THE MANCHESTER COAST

    Brooklyn Art Association:

                    THE BRIDLE PATH

1870—age 34—New York; summer in Adirondacks.
    Illustrations: in *Harper's Weekly*; *Appleton's Journal*; *The Galaxy*; *Every Saturday*; *Harper's Bazaar*.
    Book illustrations: in *Atlantic Almanac*; Whittier: *Ballads of New England*.
    Exhibited: New York, National Academy of Design:

                    WHITE MOUNTAIN WAGON
                    SKETCH FROM NATURE
                    MT. ADAMS
                    SAIL BOAT
                    SALEM HARBOUR
                    LOBSTER COVE
                    AS YOU LIKE IT
                    SAWKILL RIVER, PENNA.
                    EAGLE HEAD, MANCHESTER
                    THE WHITE MOUNTAINS
                    MANNERS & CUSTOMS OF THE SEASIDE

    New York, American Water Color Society: one painting.

1871—age 35—New York.
    Illustrations: in *Every Saturday*.
    Book illustrations: in Byrant's *Song of the Sower*; *Winter Poems*.

1872—age 36—New York; moved to Studio Building, 51 West Tenth St.
    Illustrations: in *Harper's Weekly*.
    Book illustration: in Bryant's *Story of the Fountain*.
    Exhibited: New York, National Academy of Design:

                    THE MILL
                    THE COUNTRY SCHOOL
                    CROSSING THE PASTURE
                    A RAINY DAY IN CAMP
                    COUNTRY STORE

1873—age 37—New York; summer in Gloucester, Massachusetts. (From 1873 through 1877 Homer's mother exhibited watercolors
        of flowers and plants at the Brooklyn Art Association.)
    Illustrations: in *Harper's Weekly*.

1874—age 38—New York; summer in Adirondacks.
Illustrations: in *Harper's Weekly*.
Book illustration: in Lowell's *The Courtin'*.
Exhibited: New York, National Academy of Design:

SCHOOL TIME

GIRL

SUNDAY MORNING

DAD'S COMING

1875—age 39—New York; summer in York, Maine, and in Virginia.
Illustrations: in *Harper's Weekly* and in *Harper's Bazaar*.
Book illustration: in *Larcom's Childhood Songs*.
Exhibited: New York, National Academy of Design:

LANDSCAPE

MILKING TIME

THE COURSE OF TRUE LOVE

UNCLE NED AT HOME

Brooklyn Art Association; American Water Color Society: 24 watercolors and drawings.
New York, American Water Color Society: 32 watercolors and drawings.

1876—age 40—New York.
Book illustration: in Bryant & Gay: *Popular History of the U.S.*
Exhibited: New York, National Academy of Design:

THE OLD BOAT

OVER THE HILLS

FORAGING

CATTLE PIECE

A FAIR WIND

New York, Metropolitan Museum:

PRISONERS FROM THE FRONT

New York, American Water Color Society: 14 watercolors.
Brooklyn Art Association:

SUNNY MORNING

Philadelphia, Centennial Exposition: 4 watercolors.

SNAP THE WHIP

THE AMERICAN TYPE

1877—age 41—New York; a founding member of the Tile Club.
Exhibited: New York, National Academy of Design:

ANSWERING THE HORN

LANDSCAPE

New York, American Water Color Society: 5 watercolors.
Brooklyn Art Association:

OTTER SIGNS

1878—age 42—New York; summer at Houghton Farm, Hurley, New York.
Book illustration: in Longfellow: *Excelsior*.
Exhibited: New York, National Academy of Design:

MORNING

SHALL I TELL YOUR FORTUNE?

A FRESH MORNING

TWO GUIDES

WATERMELON BOYS

IN THE FIELD

Paris Exposition:

SNAP THE WHIP

ON THE BRIGHT SIDE

VISIT FROM THE OLD MISTRESS

SUNDAY MORNING

COUNTRY SCHOOL

1879—age 43—New York; summer in West Townsend, Massachusetts.
     Exhibited: New York, National Academy of Design:

                         SUNDOWN
                         UPLAND COTTON
                         SHEPHERDESS OF HOUGHTON FARM

          New York, American Water Color Society: 29 watercolors and drawings.

1880—age 44—New York; summer in Gloucester, Massachusetts.
     Book illustrations: in Appleton's *Summer Book for Woodside & Seaside.*
     Exhibited: New York, National Academy of Design:

                         SUMMER
                         VISIT FROM THE OLD MISTRESS
                         CAMPFIRE
                         SUNDAY MORNING

1881—age 45—England, in the spring, stayed at Tynemouth.
     Exhibited: New York, American Water Color Society: 23 watercolors and drawings.

1882—age 46—England; returned to U.S. in November.
     Exhibited: London, Royal Academy:

                         HARK THE LARK

          New York, American Water Color Society: 2 watercolors.
          Brooklyn Art Association:

                         FISHERMAN'S DAUGHTER
                         FISHING FLEET, NEW CASTLE, ENGLAND

1883—age 47—New York; temporary address 80 East Washington Square, New York University Building; summer at Atlantic
          City, New Jersey, and later settled at Prouts Neck, Maine.
     Exhibited: New York, National Academy of Design:

                         THE COMING AWAY OF THE GALE

          New York, American Water Color Society: 4 watercolors.
          Boston, Doll & Richards: a group of Tynemouth watercolors.

1884—age 48—Prouts Neck; to the Grand Banks with the fishing fleet; winter to Nassau; mother died April 27.
     Exhibited: New York, National Academy of Design:

                         THE LIFE LINE

          New York, American Water Color Society: 2 watercolors.

1885—age 49—Prouts Neck; winter in Nassau and Cuba.
     Exhibited: Pittsburgh, Carnegie Institute:

                         BANKS FISHERMEN
                         FOG WARNING

1886—age 50—Prouts Neck; winter in Florida.
     Exhibited: Boston, Doll & Richards: 15 Bahama and Cuba watercolors.

1887—age 51—Prouts Neck.
     Illustrations: Civil War sketches for *Century* magazine.
     Exhibited: New York, National Academy of Design:

                         UNDERTOW

          New York, American Water Color Society: 2 watercolors.
          Pittsburgh, Carnegie Institute:

                         HARK THE LARK
                         UNDERTOW

1888—age 52—Prouts Neck.
     Exhibited: New York, National Academy of Design:

                         EIGHT BELLS (lent by T. B. Clarke)

          New York, American Water Color Society: 6 watercolors.
          Philadelphia, Pennsylvania Academy:

                         UNDERTOW

1889—age 53—Prouts Neck; summer and fall in Adirondacks. From this year through 1905, Homer did not exhibit at the National
          Academy of Design in New York.

1890—age 54—Prouts Neck; winter in Florida.
     Exhibited: Boston, Doll & Richards: a group of Adirondack watercolors.

1891—age 55—Prouts Neck; summer and fall in Adirondacks.
    Exhibited: New York, Reichards: two Maine Coast marines.

        SIGNAL OF DISTRESS

        SUMMER NIGHT

    New York, American Water Color Society: one watercolor.
    Pittsburgh, Carnegie Institute:

        HUNTSMAN AND DOGS

1892—age 56—Prouts Neck; summer and fall in Adirondacks.
    Exhibited: Pittsburgh, Carnegie Institute:

        HOUND AND HUNTER

1893—age 57—Prouts Neck; to Chicago to visit the Columbian Exposition.
    Exhibited: Chicago Exposition:

        THE CARNIVAL

        A GREAT GALE (gold medal)

        CAMPFIRE

        EIGHT BELLS

        MARCH WIND

        COAST IN WINTER

        TWO GUIDES

        SUNSET

        HOUND & HUNTER

        RETURN FROM HUNT

        SUNLIGHT ON THE COAST

        LOST ON THE GRAND BANKS

        FOG WARNING

        HERRING FISHING

        COAST IN WINTER

    Philadelphia, Pennsylvania Academy: watercolors.

        FOX HUNT

    Pittsburgh, Carnegie Institute:

        THE GALE

        FOX HUNT

1894—age 58—Prouts Neck; summer in Adirondacks.
    Exhibited: Boston, Doll & Richards: a group of Adirondack and marine watercolors.
    Pittsburgh, Carnegie Institute:

        FISHER GIRL

        HIGH CLIFF

1895—age 59—Prouts Neck; summer and fall in Canada.
    Exhibited: Philadelphia, Pennsylvania Academy:

        NORTHEASTER

        MOONLIGHT, WOODS ISLAND LIGHT

        STORMBEATEN

    Pittsburgh, Carnegie Institute:

        CANNON ROCK

1896—age 60—Prouts Neck.
    Exhibited: Philadelphia, Pennsylvania Academy:

        SUNSET, SACO BAY (awarded gold medal)

    Pittsburgh, Carnegie Institute:

        THE LOOKOUT

        SUNSET, SACO BAY

        MAINE COAST

        TWO GUIDES

        THE WRECK (awarded gold medal and $5,000 purchase prize)

1897—age 61—Prouts Neck; summer in Canada.
 Exhibited: New York, Society of American Artists:

MARINE

THE LOOKOUT

SACO BAY

  Pittsburgh, Carnegie Institute:

FLIGHT OF WILD GEESE

LIGHT ON THE SEA

1898—age 62—Prouts Neck; summer in Canada, winter in Nassau; father died August 22.
 Exhibited: New York, Union League Club: 25 paintings from the T. B. Clarke Collection.

1899—age 63—Prouts Neck; winter in Bermuda and Nassau; Clarke Collection sold at auction.
 Exhibited: Philadelphia, Pennsylvania Academy:

THE GULF STREAM

HIGH SEAS

  Boston, Doll & Richards: 27 watercolors of Quebec.
  Pittsburgh, Carnegie Institute: 27 watercolors of Quebec.

THE GULF STREAM

SEARCHLIGHT, HARBOR ENTRANCE, SANTIAGO DE CUBA

1900—age 64—Prouts Neck; summer in Adirondacks.
 Exhibited: Paris exposition:

FOX HUNT

COAST OF MAINE

THE LOOKOUT

SUMMER NIGHT (awarded gold medal and bought for the Luxembourg, but grand prizes went to Sargent and Whistler)

  Philadelphia, Pennsylvania Academy:

SIGNAL OF DISTRESS

  Pittsburgh, Carnegie Institute:

ON A LEE SHORE

  New York, Society of American Artists:

HIGH SEAS

1901—age 65—Prouts Neck; winter in Bermuda(?).
 Exhibited: Philadelphia, Pennsylvania Academy:

NORTHEASTER

FLIGHT OF WILD GEESE

  Boston Art Club:

FOG

  New York, Society of American Artists:

WEST POINT

EASTERN POINT

  Buffalo, Pan American Exposition: group of watercolors, awarded gold medal.

1902—age 66—Prouts Neck; summer in Canada.
 Exhibited: New York, Society of American Artists:

NORTHEASTER

  Philadelphia, Pennsylvania Academy:

EASTERN POINT

THE UNRULY CALF

  Charleston, South Carolina, exposition:

CANNON ROCK (awarded gold medal)

1903—age 67—Prouts Neck; winter in Florida.
 Exhibited: New York, Society of American Artists:

EARLY MORNING

CANNON ROCK

  Philadelphia, Pennsylvania Academy:

EARLY MORNING

EIGHT BELLS

1904—age 68—Prouts Neck; winter in Florida.
    Exhibited: Boston Art Club:

BELOW ZERO

      St. Louis exposition:

EARLY MORNING

WEATHERBEATEN (awarded gold medal)

1905—age 69—Prouts Neck; winter in Atlantic City, New Jersey.
    Exhibited: Philadelphia, Pennsylvania Academy:

KISSING THE MOON

      New York, American Water Color Society: one watercolor.

1906—age 70—Prouts Neck; long illness in summer, no new work fall 1905-8.
    Exhibited: London, International Society of Sculptors, Painters and Gravers:

SIGNAL OF DISTRESS

      Philadelphia, Pennsylvania Academy:

LONG BRANCH

      New York, National Academy of Design:

THE GULF STREAM

1907—age 71—Prouts Neck.
    Exhibited: Philadelphia, Pennsylvania Academy:

HIGH CLIFF

      Pittsburgh, Carnegie Institute:

EARLY EVENING

1908—age 72—Prouts Neck; ill with paralytic stroke in May; summer in Adirondacks.
    Exhibited: New York, National Academy of Design:

WEST WIND

HOUND AND HUNTER

      Philadelphia, Pennsylvania Academy:

SEARCHLIGHT, HARBOR ENTRANCE, SANTIAGO DE CUBA

1909—age 73—Prouts Neck.
    Exhibited: American Water Color Society: 5 watercolors and drawings.
      Philadelphia, Pennsylvania Academy:

EARLY EVENING

1910—age 74—Prouts Neck.
    Exhibited: Berlin and Munich, American Art Exposition:

THE GULF STREAM

THE LOOKOUT

      New York, American Water Color Society: 2 drawings.
      New York, National Academy of Design:

BELOW ZERO

WEATHERBEATEN

CAMPFIRE

SUNSET, SACO BAY

HIGH CLIFF

WEST WIND

      Philadelphia, Pennsylvania Academy:

RIGHT AND LEFT

Homer died at Prouts Neck, September 29.

INDEX OF ILLUSTRATIONS

NOTE: *In giving measurements of the paintings* height *comes first. The measurements are only approximate, but they will give the reader an idea of the scale of the original painting. A date given in parenthesis (1860) indicates that the artist did not put a date on the painting, and that this date is only approximate.*

CANOE IN RAPIDS

Watercolor 13½ x 20½ inches
Signed: Homer 1895
Metropolitan Museum of Art
Gift of George A. Hearn

CAPE TRINITY, SAGUENAY RIVER

Oil 28½ x 48½ inches
Signed: Homer (1904)
Collection of Mr. Alastair B. Martin

CAPRICE IN PURPLE AND GOLD:
THE GOLDEN SCREEN

J. A. McN. Whistler
Freer Gallery of Art, Smithsonian
    Institution, Washington, D.C.

THE CARNIVAL

Oil 20 x 30 inches
Signed: Winslow Homer N.A. 1877
Metropolitan Museum of Art
Lazarus Fund

CAVALRY OFFICER

Drawing
Cooper Union Museum

CAVALRY OFFICER (sketch)

Drawing
Cooper Union Museum

CAVALRYMAN (sketch)

Drawing
Cincinnati Art Museum

CHANNEL BASS

Watercolor 11 x 19 inches
Signed: W.H. 1904
Metropolitan Museum of Art
George A. Hearn Fund

LE CHANT D' AMOUR

Edward Burne-Jones
Oil 45 x 61½ inches
Signed: E.B.J.
Metropolitan Museum of Art
Punnett Fund

CHILDREN PLAYING UNDER A
GLOUCESTER WHARF

Watercolor 8 x 13½ inches
Signed: Homer 1880
Museum of Fine Arts, Boston

CHRISTMAS BOXES IN CAMP—
CHRISTMAS 1861

Illustration from *Harper's Weekly*,
    January 4, 1862
Metropolitan Museum of Art

CONCH DIVERS

Watercolor 14 x 20 inches
Signed: Homer 85
Minneapolis Institute of Arts
Dunwoody Fund

COTTON PICKERS

Oil 24 x 38 inches
Signed: Winslow Homer N.A. 1876
Collection of Mr. and Mrs. James Cox
    Brady

THE COUNTRY SCHOOL

Oil 21 x 38 inches
Signed: Winslow Homer—1871
City Art Museum of St. Louis

COURSING THE HARE

Oil 15½ x 28½ inches
Collection of Mr. and Mrs. Paul Mellon

CROQUET PLAYERS

Drawing, black chalk 11½ x 10 inches
Signed: W.H. (dated on reverse 1866)
Metropolitan Museum of Art
Fletcher Fund

CROQUET SCENE

Oil 15½ x 26 inches
Signed: Winslow Homer 66
Art Institute of Chicago
Friends of American Art Collection

DEER DRINKING

Watercolor 13½ x 19½ inches
Signed: Homer 1892
Collection of Mr. and Mrs. Courtlandt P.
    Dixon

DEFIANCE: INVITING A SHOT BEFORE
PETERSBURG, VIRGINIA, 1864

Oil 12 x 18 inches
Signed: Homer 1864
Detroit Institute of Arts

DIAMOND SHOAL

Watercolor 13½ x 21½ inches
Signed: Homer 1905
International Business Machines
    Corporation

THE DINNER HORN

Oil 12 x 14 inches
Signed: Homer 1873
Detroit Institute of Arts

DRIFTWOOD

Oil 24 x 28 inches
Signed: Homer 1909
Collection of Dr. and Mrs. S. Emlen
    Stokes

EARLY MORNING AFTER A STORM
AT SEA

Oil 30 x 50 inches
Signed: Homer 1902
Cleveland Museum of Art
J. H. Wade Collection

EAST HAMPTON, LONG ISLAND

Oil 10 x 21½ inches
Signed: W.H. 1874
Collection of Mr. William Roerick

EASTERN POINT LIGHT

Watercolor 9½ x 13½ inches
Princeton University Art Museum

EASTERN SHORE

Lithographic reproduction of a
    watercolor
Metropolitan Museum of Art

EIGHT BELLS

Oil 25 x 30 inches
Signed: Winslow Homer 1886
Addison Gallery of American Art,
    Phillips Academy, Andover,
    Massachusetts

EIGHT BELLS

Etching
Metropolitan Museum of Art

EVENING ON THE BEACH

Drawing 8½ x 15 inches
Signed: Homer 71
Collection of Mrs. Thomas Hitchcock

FISHERFOLK ON THE BEACH
AT TYNEMOUTH

Watercolor 13½ x 18½ inches
Signed: Homer 1881
Addison Gallery of American Art,
    Phillips Academy, Andover,
    Massachusetts

FISHERMEN BEACHING A DORY AT
TYNEMOUTH, ENGLAND

Drawing
Signed: Homer
Cooper Union Museum

FISHERMEN ON SHORE

Drawing
Signed: Homer 1884
Montclair Art Museum

FISHERWOMEN

Drawing
Signed: Homer 1882
Metropolitan Museum of Art

FISHING BOATS, KEY WEST

Watercolor 13½ x 21½ inches
Signed: W. Homer 1903
Metropolitan Museum of Art
Lazarus Fund

THE FISHING PARTY, STUDY FOR

Drawing
Cooper Union Museum

FLAMBOROUGH HEAD, ENGLAND

Drawing
Signed: Winslow Homer 1882
Art Institute of Chicago
Ryerson Collection

HOUSES OF PARLIAMENT

Watercolor 12 x 19 inches
Signed: Homer 1881
Collection of Mr. Joseph Hirschhorn

HUDSON RIVER, LOGGING

Watercolor 14 x 21 inches
Signed: Homer (1897?)
Corcoran Gallery of Art

HUNTER IN THE ADIRONDACKS

Watercolor
Signed:
Fogg Museum of Art, Harvard University
Grenville L. Winthrop Collection

HUNTSMAN AND DOGS

Oil 28 x 48 inches
Signed: Winslow Homer 1891
Philadelphia Museum of Art
William L. Elkins Collection

HURRICANE, BAHAMAS

Watercolor 14½ x 21 inches
(1898)
Metropolitan Museum of Art
Lazarus Fund

IN THE MOUNTAINS

Oil 24 x 38 inches
Brooklyn Museum

THE INITIALS

Oil 16 x 12 inches
Signed: Homer 64
Collection of Mr. and Mrs. Lawrence A.
 Fleischman

INSIDE THE BAR

Watercolor 15½ x 28½ inches
Signed: Homer 83
Metropolitan Museum of Art
Gift of Mrs. Bartlett Arkell in memory
 of her husband

INTERNATIONAL TEA PARTY

Drawing
Cooper Union Museum

KISSING THE MOON

Oil 30 x 40 inches
Signed: Homer 1904
Addison Gallery of American Art,
 Phillips Academy, Andover
Candace C. Stimson Bequest

A LADY (illustration)

John Everett Millais
New York Public Library

LEAPING TROUT

Watercolor 14 x 20 inches
Signed: Homer (1889?)
Museum of Fine Arts, Boston

THE LETTER HOME

Lithograph from *Campaign Sketches*
New York Public Library

LIE IN CAMP—PART 1

(a series of twelve comic cards)
Lithograph
Metropolitan Museum of Art
Gift of J. R. Burdick

LIFE IN CAMP—PART 2

(second series of twelve
comic cards)
Lithograph
Metropolitan Museum of Art
Gift of J. R. Burdick

THE LIFE LINE

Oil 29 x 45 inches
Signed: Winslow Homer 1884
Philadelphia Museum of Art
William L. Elkins Collection

A LIGHT ON THE SEA

Oil 28 x 48 inches
Signed: Homer 1897
Corcoran Gallery of Art

LONG BRANCH, NEW JERSEY

Oil 15 x 21½ inches
Signed: Winslow Homer 1869
Museum of Fine Arts, Boston

LOOKING OVER THE CLIFF

Watercolor 20½ x 13½ inches
Signed: Winslow Homer 1882
Plainfield Public Library, Plainfield,
 New Jersey

THE LOOKOUT—"ALL'S WELL"

Oil 40 x 30 inches
Signed: Homer 1896
Museum of Fine Arts, Boston

LOST ON THE GRAND BANKS

Oil 28 x 48 inches
Signed: Winslow Homer 1885
Collection of Mr. John S. Broome

LUMBERING IN WINTER

Illustration from *Every Saturday*, Vol. II,
 n.s. January 28, 1871
Metropolitan Museum of Art

MAINE COAST

Oil 30 x 44 inches
Signed: Homer 1895
Metropolitan Museum of Art
Gift of George A. Hearn in memory of
 Arthur H. Hearn

MAKING HAVELOCKS FOR THE
VOLUNTEERS

Illustration from *Harper's Weekly*,
 Vol. V, June 29, 1861
Metropolitan Museum of Art

McCLELLAN'S CAVALRY

Drawing
Cooper Union Museum

MENDING THE NETS

Watercolor 27½ x 19½ inches
Signed: Winslow Homer 1882
Collection of Mr. and Mrs. Solton Engle

MENDING THE NETS

Etching
Metropolitan Museum of Art

MOONLIGHT—WOOD'S ISLAND LIGHT

Oil 30½ x 40 inches
Signed: W.H. 1894
Metropolitan Museum of Art
Gift of George A. Hearn in memory of
 Arthur H. Hearn

MILKING TIME

Oil 24 x 38 inches
Signed: Winslow Homer 1875
Collection of Mr. and Mrs. Solton Engle

THE MINK POND

Watercolor 14 x 21 inches
Signed:
Fogg Museum of Art, Harvard University
Grenville L. Winthrop Collection

THE MORNING BELL

Oil 24 x 38 inches
Signed: Winslow Homer (1866?)
Estate of Stephen C. Clark

MORNING GLORIES

Oil 19½ x 13½ inches
Signed: Winslow Homer 1873
Collection of Mr. and Mrs. Paul Mellon

NASSAU

Watercolor 15 x 21 inches
Signed: Homer 1899
Metropolitan Museum of Art
Lazarus Fund

NATURAL BRIDGE, NASSAU

Watercolor 14½ x 21 inches
(1898)
Metropolitan Museum of Art
Lazarus Fund

NEW ENGLAND COUNTRY SCHOOL

Oil 12 x 18 inches
Signed: Homer 1872
Addison Gallery of American Art,
 Phillips Academy, Andover

THE NEW NOVEL

Watercolor, 9½ x 20½ inches
Signed: Homer 1877
Museum of Fine Arts, Springfield,
 Massachusetts

SHOOTING THE RAPIDS,
SAGUENAY RIVER

Oil 30 x 48 inches
(1905, unfinished)
Metropolitan Museum of Art
Gift of Charles S. Homer

SHORE AND SURF, NASSAU

Watercolor 15 x 23½ inches
Signed: Homer '99
Metropolitan Museum of Art
Lazarus Fund

SHOWER BELOW THE MOUNTAIN

Hokusai
Japanese print from the series THIRTY-SIX
VIEWS OF FUJI
Metropolitan Museum of Art

THE SIGNAL OF DISTRESS

Drawing
(1890?)
Cooper Union Museum

SKATING IN CENTRAL PARK

Water color 16 x 24 inches
(1860?)
City Art Museum of St. Louis

A SKIRMISH IN THE WILDERNESS

Oil 18 x 26 inches
Signed: Homer 64
New Britain Museum of American Art,
New Britain, Connecticut

SLOOP, BERMUDA

Watercolor 15 x 21½ inches
(1899)
Metropolitan Museum of Art
Lazarus Fund

SNAP THE WHIP

Oil 22 x 36 inches
Signed: Homer 1872
Butler Institute of American Art,
Youngstown, Ohio

SNAP THE WHIP

Oil 12 x 20 inches
Signed: Homer 1872
Metropolitan Museum of Art
Gift of Christian A. Zabriskie

SNAP THE WHIP

Drawing
Cooper Union Museum
SNAP THE WHIP

Illustration from Harper's Weekly,
Vol. XVII, September 20, 1873
Metropolitan Museum of Art

SOLDIERS' HEADS

Drawing
(1863?)
Cooper Union Museum

SOLDIERS PLAYING CARDS

Lithograph from Campaign Sketches
New York Public Library

SOLDIERS (sketches)

Drawing
(1863?)
Cooper Union Museum

SOLDIERS (studies)

Drawing
(1863?)
Cooper Union Museum

THE SPONGE DIVER, BAHAMAS

Watercolor 13½ x 19 inches
Signed: Homer 1889
Museum of Fine Arts, Boston

SPRING

Watercolor 11 x 8½
Signed: Homer 1878
Collection of Mrs. George W. Headley

SPRING FARM WORK—GRAFTING

Illustration from Harper's Weekly,
Vol. XIV, April 30, 1870
Metropolitan Museum of Art

STILL LIFE: WILD DUCKS

Oil 28½ x 22½ inches
Signed: Winslow Homer 1893
Private Collection, New York

THE STORM

Oil 19½ x 35 inches
(1882?)
Denver Art Museum
Helen Dill Collection

STOWING SAILS, BAHAMAS

Watercolor 14 x 22 inches
Signed: Homer 1903
Art Institute of Chicago
Ryerson Collection

THE STRAWBERRY BED

Illustration from Our Young Folks,
Vol. IV, July 1868
Metropolitan Museum of Art

STUDIO BUILDING,

WEST 10TH STREET, NEW YORK
Photograph
New-York Historical Society

SUNDAY MORNING IN VIRGINIA

Oil 18 x 24 inches
Signed: Homer 1877
Cincinnati Art Museum

SUNLIGHT ON THE COAST

Oil 30 x 40 inches
Signed: Winslow Homer 1890
Toledo Museum of Art
Libbey Collection

SWINGING ON A BIRCH TREE

Illustration from Our Young Folks,
Vol. III, June 1867
Metropolitan Museum of Art

TAKING ON WET PROVISIONS

Watercolor 14 x 21½ inches
Signed: W.H. 1903
Metropolitan Museum of Art
Lazarus Fund

THANKSGIVING DAY, 1858

Illustration from Harper's Weekly,
Vol. II, November 27, 1858
Metropolitan Museum of Art

THORNHILL BAR

Watercolor 14 x 20 inches
Signed: W.H. 1886
Museum of Fine Arts, Boston

TO THE RESCUE

Oil 24 x 30 inches
Signed: Homer (1886)
Phillips Collection, Washington, D.C.

THE TURTLE POUND

Watercolor 15 x 21½ inches
Signed: Homer 1898
Brooklyn Museum
White Memorial Fund and A. A. Healy
Fund

TWO EQUESTRIANS (illustration)

John Everett Millais
New York Public Library

TWO GIRLS ON THE BEACH,
TYNEMOUTH

Watercolor 13½ x 19½ inches
Signed: Winslow Homer 1881
Collection of Mrs. John S. Ames

THE TWO GUIDES

Oil 24 x 40 inches
Sterling and Francine Clark Art
Institute, Williamstown, Massachusetts

TWO LADIES

Watercolor 7 x 8 inches
Signed: Homer 1880
Metropolitan Museum of Art
Given in memory of Florence B. Meyer

TWO LITTLE GIRLS

Drawing—reproduced in Sheldon's book
Hours with Arts and Artists, c. 1882
Metropolitan Museum of Art

UNDER THE COCO PALM

Watercolor 14½ x 20½ inches
Signed: Winslow Homer 1898
Fogg Museum of Art, Harvard University
Grenville L. Winthrop Collection

INDEX OF MUSEUMS
AND PRIVATE COLLECTIONS

INDEX

NOTE: *Entries in capitals refer to the pictures in the book. Entries in italics are titles referred to in the text.*

PHOTOGRAPHIC CREDITS

The color photographs reproduced in this volume
were made by the following:

Metropolitan Museum of Art